MARY BOWRING was born in Suffolk and went to school in Belgium. During the war, when she served in the WAAF, she met and married her husband who was in the army. Now she helps him run his veterinary practice and they live in the country with their son and daughter and various animals.

Her main interests are family life, books, writing and the countryside. She dislikes formal entertaining, so keeps open house for her friends – and their animals – to drop in at will.

THE ANIMALS COME FIRST

Mary Bowring

With a Foreword by Philip Wayre

FONTANA/COLLINS

First published by Collins & Harvill Press 1976
First issued in Fontana 1977

Copyright © Mary Bowring 1976

Made and printed in Great Britain by
William Collins Sons & Co. Ltd, Glasgow

Foreword

Having been concerned for over twenty years with the conservation of wild life and the care and breeding of animals in captivity, I am particularly impressed by Mrs Bowring's account of her husband's dedicated and tireless devotion to his work. Without the invaluable contribution of veterinary surgeons to the care of animals, collections such as mine could not succeed. This book is a timely reminder of our debt to the skills of our 'vets'.

Mary Bowring gives us not only a fascinating account of the day-to-day life of a vet's wife, but equally interesting and easily-assimilated information about the animals her husband treats. In a lively conversational style she writes of subjects ranging from the care of dogs, and the correct attitudes towards humanising pets, to the elephant's teeth and the terrible dangers of rabies.

As the seasons pass, Mrs Bowring introduces us to the varied, sometimes eccentric, occasionally rude people one meets in a busy practice. Invariably she treats them with kindness and tolerance.

This very readable book reveals a woman who is capable, modest and unsentimental, whose enviable relationship with her husband after 'a lightning courtship' is shown in her descriptions of domestic 'crises' concerning wedding anniversaries, decorating the house and holidays which emphasise that for the wife of a successful veterinary surgeon 'the animals must come first'. Altogether a delightful behind the scenes glimpse into the world of a busy vet.

PHILIP WAYRE
The Norfolk Wildlife Park

Chapter 1

My husband put his head round the door.

'I've got a hysterectomy coming in. Can you give me a hand in half-an-hour?'

I nodded, then turned to the woman who was trying to lure me into joining some local Society.

'You see?' I said, 'being a Vet's wife really does take up all my time.'

I don't think she believed me, although one glance at the state of my living room should have convinced her. She probably thought I was just badly organised. Well, perhaps I am. But it doesn't worry me. I haven't got time to think about it.

We live just outside a small country town in a beautiful part of Surrey in a comfortable, square house with fields at the back. The Surgery is a separate building on one side of the large garden. Waiting Room, office, store room and consulting room, they are all kept immaculate with everything in place.

This, I sometimes think, symbolises our attitude to life, where animals and their needs are of first importance. In this area, Maurice rules supreme and I am his loyal, unquestioning slave. Mind you, I make up for this by being boss in the house – an arrangement which seems to work very well.

When we bought this Practice we knew that we had reached our goal after a long, hard journey, interrupted by six years of war.

We met during that time, when Maurice was a Captain in the Royal Tank Regiment and I was a humble – well, not very humble – Corporal in the W.A.A.F. We were both reluctant blind dates, cajoled into making up a foursome by our mutual friends. It was a whirlwind romance. We got engaged at our fourth meeting and were married two months later. A fortnight together and then Maurice was sent overseas to fight in North Africa and all the way up Italy. It was one of those wartime marriages that are supposed to end in disaster. Only ours didn't.

When the War ended, Maurice received a grant of one hundred pounds a year from a grateful government and returned to the Royal Veterinary College in London where he had already done three years of the five year course.

It was difficult for him to get accustomed to studying again. He and the other ex-service people were war-hardened veterans and the students – and some of the professors – seemed like overgrown children; but everyone was understanding and, eventually, he qualified.

On the day we learnt that he was now a full blown M.R.C.V.S., we were so tired – and broke – that we never even went out to dinner to celebrate. But, as I looked at my tall husband, beginning to go grey even in his early thirties, I was so proud of him that I burst into tears.

Then came the years of gaining experience with a variety of Vets and an even greater variety of accommo-dation. During this time our first child was born. She was severely handicapped and our life was filled with sadness for eight years. Maurice, always so gentle and kind with suffering creatures, was a tower of compassionate strength and we kept our little girl as happy as possible.

2

When she died, our son was nearly two years old and we had just managed to buy our own Practice from an elderly Vet. Money was still a constant worry because the old Vet had let things go, but Maurice gradually increased the work until at last we had a thriving Practice of large and small animals.

At first he employed a girl to help in the Surgery but, when she left to get married, I took her place. I was, in fact, thrown in at the deep end. I was pregnant at the time, expecting our third child and awaiting a Caesarean operation when, one Sunday afternoon, there was an emergency.

Maurice said, 'I've got to do a Caesar on this little bitch. She's really too small to have puppies and she's in a bad state.'

He looked at me anxiously, 'I need help with the anaesthetising but . . .'

'All right,' I said, 'I'll lend a hand till she's under, then I'll disappear.'

When she was unconscious, Maurice looked at me and grinned. 'Why don't you watch?' he asked, 'it's really very simple and, perhaps, it will take away your own fears.'

He was right. I quivered a bit as he made the first incision, but soon became so interested that I forgot my own condition.

We took out five sleepy but healthy pups and I rubbed them hard with a rough towel to clean and stimulate them, then put them in a box on a hot water bottle. I gazed admiringly as Maurice stitched up the wound, sewed on the gauze to protect it and, finally, laid his patient gently down and covered her with a blanket.

3

A few hours later, she was a proud mother, her eyes glowing with adoration of the little wriggling bundles snuggling up to her.

I had a great time in hospital regaling the nurses with that story but, thankfully, our lovely new daughter did not turn out to be quins.

Chapter 2

As soon as I entered the Surgery to help Maurice with the hysterectomy he put his fingers to his lips, nodded towards the Waiting Room and led me into his office.

'Oh! dear!' I said, 'is it one of those?'

He shrugged helplessly, 'A perfectly straightforward operation on a poodle. But it belongs to Miss Dillington. She's in there now. Won't go home until it's over. Convinced "Angel" is going to die. She's said goodbye to it three times already. Just help me with the anaesthetic then you'll have to go and sit with her, otherwise she'll come bursting in here and have hysterics.'

As if to bear out what he said, a loud sobbing came from the Waiting Room and I began to feel alarmed.

'Do you think I'll be able to cope with her? She sounds in a terrible state.'

'She is, but give her a nip of this if she gets out of hand.'

Maurice went to his cupboard and put a bottle of brandy and a small glass on the desk.

'I'll just go and have another word with her whilst you get things ready. Then I'll bring her in here in case anyone else comes into the Waiting Room. Not very good for my image if they see her weeping.'

The little poodle was sitting quietly by the radiator, and I stroked her curly head.

'Hello, Angel,' I said, '*you* look calm enough, anyway.'

Earlier on, Maurice had given her a tranquilliser and she was quiet and friendly. The loud lamentation from

5

the room next door seemed to have no effect on her at all. Probably this was something she had learnt to live with.

I took the steriliser off the gas, set out the operating table and made sure that everything was to hand. Then, as I stood stroking Angel and waiting for Maurice, I thought about Miss Dillington.

She was a large, middle-aged spinster of masculine appearance which entirely belied her excessive femininity. She kept three poodles and four budgies and was one of our most neurotic clients. Having done the rounds of all the Vets in the area, she had finally settled for Maurice, much to his dismay. But he sympathised with her in that she was a lonely woman whose only real friends were her pets. To these she gave all her love and they filled her empty life.

I, too, was sorry for her but I don't think she quite trusted me. I had once been rather sharp with her when she had tried to get Maurice – who was down with 'flu at the time – to go to see one of her budgies in the middle of the night for something quite trivial. So our relations were rather strained and, although she was always very polite, I knew that she regarded me as a dragon-like barrier between her and the man to whom she entrusted her beloved pets.

Suddenly I realised that the sobbing was coming from the office and the next moment Maurice appeared. He took out his handkerchief and wiped his forehead. 'I've taken her through by the side door; now, let's get this over.'

Quickly unfastening Angel's lead, he lifted her on to the table and I put my arm round her to keep her still. He pulled out her foreleg and I gripped it behind the elbow

6

and pressed to bring up the radial vein. He clipped the hair off the area and slipped in the needle. A few seconds later Angel went limp. We turned her on to her back, attached each leg to the table and pulled out her tongue so that it hung to one side.

'Are you sure you can manage without me?' I asked, and he nodded.

There was a sound of movement from the room behind us and he said, 'If she comes in here I'll have to abandon the operation, so, hurry.'

Opening the door, I nearly collided with Miss Dillington. She grabbed my arm.

'What's happening? Is anything wrong?'

'Good gracious, no,' I said, trying to make my voice as light as possible and leading her gently back to her chair, I sat down beside her.

Her face was blotchy with tears and she looked utterly distraught, so, picking up the bottle, I said, 'My husband suggests you have a drop of this to make you feel better.'

She stared at me suspiciously but eventually took the glass. 'Perhaps he's right,' she said, and drank it in one gulp.

'Tell me about Angel, she seems exceptionally intelligent.' To my relief I saw that I had struck the right note and for nearly half-an-hour, I listened to a string of anecdotes which covered Angel's life from the moment she was born.

Every now and then, Miss Dillington would pause for breath and half rise from her chair as she remembered what was going on behind the door, but I poured a little more brandy into the glass and, each time, she knocked it back unthinkingly. It was only when her speech became a little slurred that I realised I was rather overdoing the First Aid but, just then, I heard the tap running and knew that Maurice was washing his hands. The operation was over.

Miss Dillington said carefully, 'That brandy has done me good. I think I'll have just a teeny drop more, if I may.'

She held out her glass but I replied hastily, 'My husband will be here in a moment. It's all over.'

I couldn't have chosen a more unfortunate phrase, because she stared at me in sudden horror and great tears poured down her flushed cheeks.

'All over,' she said dully, 'it's all over.'

'No! No!' I hastened to reassure her, 'I mean he's finished operating. Angel will be all right now.'

Then, with a sudden chill at my heart, I wondered if I had spoken too soon. Things can go wrong and Angel was no longer young and grossly overweight.

But all was well. The door opened and Maurice stood there beaming.

Miss Dillington stood up, swayed majestically towards him and collapsed against his white coat. I left him to it and went into the Surgery to wash the instruments.

Angel was lying by the radiator covered with a blanket. The twitching movements showed that she was slowly coming round and I breathed a sigh of relief.

When Miss Dillington came out of the office she was walking very carefully and on seeing her poodle, she turned to Maurice, her heavy face alight with gratitude. 'I can't thank you enough,' she said, rather incoherently, and then, gracefully, slid to the floor beside Angel.

Somehow, we got her up into a chair and watched anxiously for signs of life. She was making funny little bubbling noises and I looked at Maurice in terror.

'It's all right,' he said, grinning broadly, 'she's just snoring. I'd better drive her home.'

He went into the office, picked up the brandy bottle and looked at it ruefully, 'Not much profit for me today!'

Not many of our clients get as worked up about their animals as Miss Dillington. Some, indeed, are so happy-go-lucky that they ignore danger signals.

A young couple brought in an Alsatian puppy about four months old. A beautiful animal but wild and untrained. As soon as they came into the Surgery the dog slipped his lead and dodged us from corner to corner of the room, barking madly and thoroughly enjoying the game. The young man and his wife seemed to think this was hilarious but, with the Waiting Room full of clients, Maurice was in no mood to share in the fun.

We finally trapped the dog by sheer weight of numbers and lifted him on to the table. Holding on grimly, I noticed that Maurice was looking puzzled. He began feeling the dog's tummy and seemed to be listening intently, a difficult task with the constant barking from his patient and appreciative chuckles from the owners.

'There's nothing wrong with him,' said the man, 'we just want you to cut his toe-nails – they're a bit long.'

His wife giggled, 'Death to my tights. He's a proper little terror.'

Maurice said nothing but, taking a piece of tape, he tied it round the dog's nose, effectively stopping the noise.

'No need to do that,' said the man, a trifle scornfully, 'Rex won't bite you.'

9

Maurice said to me, 'Let go of him for a moment, will you? I'm holding him.'

To my surprise, he gave the dog a shake and then, in spite of the gasp of indignation from the owners, I heard a distinct rattling sound.

'There!' he said, 'that's what I heard just now. Listen . . .' he shook the animal a little harder and, this time, the rattle was unmistakable.

'Oh! That's nothing,' said the girl, 'he's been doing that for ages. He just loves eating pebbles – they don't hurt him. It's just one of his tricks, he's a right little comic, he is.'

'There's nothing comic about this,' said Maurice gravely. 'Does he swallow anything else?'

'Anything he can get hold of,' said the man cheerfully, 'it's no use telling him to drop something when he's got it in his mouth. He just seems to laugh at you. Has us in fits, he does.'

'You won't be the only ones in fits if this goes on,' said Maurice, 'he's got to have an operation before these things cause serious trouble.'

At last the young couple quietened down and Maurice explained carefully what would happen if nothing were done. 'Sooner or later, Rex will develop acute gastritis accompanied by vomiting. He will be in severe pain and, depending on what he has swallowed, there could be a rupture of the stomach which would be fatal.'

They brought him next day to be operated on and arranged to pick him up in the evening.

Rex swallowed the tranquilliser as joyfully as he had swallowed everything else and gradually calmed down. By the time we were ready for him he was easy to handle and, almost as soon as the anaesthetic was injected, he lay peacefully unconscious, stretched out on the table.

I watched with interest as Maurice made an incision about four inches long in the skin, then cut through the muscle into the abdomen. He brought the stomach up into the mouth of the wound as far as it would come. In order to avoid any of the contents of the bag going into the abdominal cavity, he packed it round with swabs. Another incision, this time into the stomach itself and, taking the artery forceps from me, he clamped them on to the edges to keep them folded back.

Then he began to delve. In amazement I watched as he laid his findings on the table. I began counting aloud.

'Seventeen, no, eighteen beer bottle tops, two tiddly winks, a coat button, six nails, a piece of string – it's about a foot long – three pieces of a sort of sheet tin, a piece of coal and a piece of bone. Oh! And another coat button – a big one, too.'

A final rout around to make sure nothing was left behind and Maurice took off the forceps and I handed him the suturing needle threaded with gut. Soon everything was neatly stitched together again, the wound covered with a roll of gauze and the operation was over.

'A canine litter bin,' said Maurice and, picking up the treasure trove, he laid it out on a side table. 'I've taken some odd things out of animals in my time but this collection beats the lot.'

He looked up from arranging the beer bottle tops in a pattern, 'Do you know, there isn't a single pebble here. So much for that couple's powers of observation. Do you suppose they throw everything on the floor in their house?'

By the time Rex's owners came in the evening, he had recovered from the anaesthetic and, although, naturally, still very dopy, was none the worse for the operation.

'He'll grow out of this habit of his, eventually,' Maurice told them, 'but, meantime, you simply mustn't leave things lying around. And you must train him to be obedient so that, when he does pick up something, he will drop it on command. I'll look in tomorrow just to make sure he's going on all right and I'll take the stitches out in ten days' time. By the way,' he smiled at them as they went towards the door, 'I'll keep this collection if you don't mind. I think I'll start a museum.'

Chapter 3

As a Vet's wife, I have learnt never to plan far ahead, never to count on anything and, above all, never to be surprised if everything falls through at the last moment. Consequently, the problem of arranging our summer holiday is a very real one.

Sometimes, in the autumn and right through the winter, we plan recklessly, vague as to the details but confident we will do something different this time. We'll take a month. We'll go on a fishing holiday, or what about a caravan, or camping, or shall we go abroad? We never mention the great difficulty of getting a Locum – we'll worry about that later.

And we do. As spring approaches our concern grows. The advertisements keep reminding us, our friends are all getting booked up – if we don't soon get someone to hold the fort for us it will be too late to get in anywhere.

Maurice, always loath to hand over his Practice to a stranger, tends to avoid the subject and, in the end, I am forced to pin him down.

First of all, I have to find the time and place in which to have a quiet, uninterrupted discussion. Almost an impossibility in our household where the telephone, besides being our bread and butter, is often death to any absorbing conversation.

This year I was resolved to get organised well in advance. I would talk it over with Maurice next time I went out with him on his calls.

Two days a week, Mrs Dixon comes to help me in the house and, having been with us for several years, she is expert at dealing with telephone calls. So I often take a busman's holiday and one of my favourite outings is going with Maurice on his weekly inspection of the animals at the local Zoo.

One day, as soon as we drew up outside the main office, George, the Superintendent, appeared.

'Am I glad to see you!' he said. 'The Malayan sunbear has a prolapse. Unfortunately, we've run out of bulbs for the dart gun and the new lot won't come till tomorrow.'

'Oh! Lord! That'll be a bit tricky,' Maurice made a face, 'better start right away.'

I got out of the car and walked with the two men towards the cage. 'You'll be careful, won't you?' I said.

The Superintendent grinned, 'Did you ever meet a Vet who wasn't? It's us poor devils who take the risks.'

'That's a debatable point,' retorted my husband, 'it's one thing to feed an animal and quite another to stick needles in its behind.'

The female bear was lying down in a corner of the cage. She was small and black with a short coat and didn't look very dangerous. But I knew that these animals are very aggressive and react like lightning to anything unpleasant.

Her mate stood nearby, watchfully on guard and, to my dismay, George said, 'Not worth the trouble of getting him into another cage. We'll keep an eye on him.'

Two keepers came up and a small crowd of spectators gathered round. Maurice opened his bag, took out a syringe and measured up an injection. 'Right!' he said.

George unlocked the cage, he and one of the keepers rushed in and flung themselves on to the bear, holding her down, whilst the other man, armed with a long broom, kept the male at a distance. Then, as calmly as though he were injecting a cow, Maurice planted the needle in the bear's back leg.

The male was growling loudly but seemed to understand that the odds were too much against him.

I sighed with relief and relaxed, but, at that moment, the female whipped round and took a vicious swipe at Maurice, missing his face by a few inches. The spectators, appreciative of the fact that they were getting something extra for their money, crowded round and a fat lady, holding a large ice cream cornet, discussed the situation with her family.

'Poor thing. Don't seem right, do it, treating it like that. Cruel, I call it.'

Her husband, a little man carrying a large baby, said, 'It's only an injection, Doris. Got to 'ave it. Make it better, see?'

'Can't see nothing wrong wiv it meself,' said the fat lady. 'Cor! Listen to that growling!' She turned and dragged forward a small boy dressed in dirty jeans and a cowboy hat. ''Ere, Alfie. Come and see what they're doing to that poor bear.'

The men relinquished their hold on the animal and got quickly out of the cage.

'Half-an-hour,' said Maurice, looking at his watch, 'she'll be pretty dopy by then and I'll be able to get to work on her.'

Our next stop was outside the elephants' enclosure where Betty, the new Indian elephant, was roaming up and down. Barbara, her predecessor, a very friendly animal, had died a few months before and I remembered how Maurice had fought for her life. Everything possible had been done but to no avail. She was the unlucky victim of the public's stupidity, having been given some rubbish which had led to her death.

Even now, as we stood watching, a youth was offering Betty something. It looked like a bun and was probably harmless enough but, in his other hand, he held a plastic bag and the elephant's trunk was waving towards it.

'Can't you read the notices?' George demanded, and the youth turned in surprise.

'I'm only giving it stale cakes. It likes them – had three already.' He held up the bag and the elephant reached out and would have had it if George hadn't knocked it aside.

' 'Ere! Wotcher doing?' the youth shouted angrily as the cakes scattered on the ground, but George was not standing any more.

'Look!' he said, pointing to the large notice fastened to the railings, 'it says: PLEASE DO NOT FEED THESE ANIMALS. We don't put that up for fun. The last elephant died because someone like you let it have something harmful. Now, if I catch you at it again, I'll have you thrown out of here.'

The youth shrugged his shoulders and ambled away, muttering to himself, and George turned to Maurice. 'We're always coming up against this, some of them get really nasty, too. We're hoping to get a baby elephant about nine months old to keep Betty company so we'll have to put up another barrier. Even then,' he added gloomily, 'people will throw things in when the keepers aren't around.'

We walked further along the side of the enclosure with

Betty following us and, suddenly, George shouted 'Look out! She's going to have her revenge.'

Too late I realised what was happening. The elephant was working her trunk round and round and then, just as Maurice and George dodged, I received a large squirt of mucus all down my shoulder, much to the onlookers' hilarity.

George produced a large rag and rubbed me down. 'It's her latest trick,' he grinned, looking fondly at his charge, 'you can't blame her. It was really me she was aiming at and I wouldn't mind betting she'll get me eventually. She won't forget that in a hurry.'

'Never mind,' said Maurice consolingly, 'just thank your lucky stars it wasn't a llama.'

I looked at him questioningly.

'They have a charming habit of ejecting the contents of their stomach at you,' he said, 'I was treating one the other day. It was off its food and running a bit of a temperature so I was giving it an injection. We'd got it jammed against a wall but, just as I got the needle in, it sprayed me – whoosh! Half-digested food with a strong smell of vomit. What's more, they go on doing it as long as there is anything left in the stomach. Not my favourite patients at all. Talking of favourites,' he added, turning to George, 'let's go and see how the lion cubs are getting on.'

Lorna the lioness had two male cubs, adorable big kittens with huge feet and sharp claws. As we stood admiring them, George explained, 'Lions are good family animals, unlike tigers. Soon these will go into the enclosure with their mother and will meet their father for the first time. As soon as Lorna allows him to get near them, Leo will lick them over and let them play all around him.'

'I'll give them their injection against feline enteritis tomorrow,' said Maurice. He looked at his watch, 'I think we'd better get back to that sunbear now.'

She was lying unconscious on the floor of the cage and, this time, it was only a question of keeping the male at bay. Maurice knelt down and began working the exposed bowel back inside. The whole thing took about twenty minutes and, when, at last, he came out, the crowd had gathered again.

'I think she'll be O.K. now,' he said to George, 'I've got it all back in place. I'll have another look at her tomorrow to make sure she's all right.'

As he stood washing his hands at the nearest tap, he was the centre of a crowd of admiring children, much to his embarrassment.

He grinned at George. 'I'll certainly be glad when that hospital you're building for me is ready. I feel rather like an animal in a cage myself with all these kids gazing at me.'

George looked across at a building in the distance. 'It won't be long now, it'll make a big difference to all of us. It's very difficult if you have a sick animal out in the open. People go round complaining that they're not being properly looked after. As if we'd be likely to neglect them,' he added indignantly, 'quite apart from the fact that these animals are extremely valuable, we get very fond of them. Wouldn't be doing the job if we didn't.'

We continued our tour and Maurice studied the camels, sea lions, the large apes, the monkeys, the hippo, the zebras, the giraffe which had recently had a baby and all the other species which made up the Zoo's fifteen hundred inhabitants.

As he discussed their problems with George, I marvelled as I so often do at the knowledge a Vet must possess. The anatomy and digestive arrangements of all these creatures, the particular ailments to which many of them are subject and the right treatment to be carried out in such difficult circumstances.

We ended up at the leopards' enclosure. The grassy paddock was wired in over the top to stop these high climbing cats from escaping.

Maurice called, 'Sue, Sue, come on, Sue,' and a young leopard came up to the bars and rubbed herself against them whilst he stroked her back.

She had known Maurice since she was born. I remembered him picking her up and playing with her but, although she was still friendly up to a point, she was becoming more dangerous as she grew older. It wouldn't be long before all the petting had to end.

'She's got a nasty abscess on her face,' George told me, pointing to her cheek where I could see an ugly hole oozing with pus. 'She was bitten by one of the other leopards.'

'It's not healing with antibiotics in her drinking water,' said Maurice, 'I'll have to open it up. I'll leave it till tomorrow when you've got those bulbs for the gun. I must "dart" her with a long-acting anaesthetic. Then I'll drain and cauterise it and pack it round with antibiotics. What do you think she weighs now? About ninety pounds?'

'Near enough,' said George.

I knew this query about the weight was in order to ascertain the dose of anaesthetic to put in the barrel of the dart which is shot into the animal by the 'Cap-Chur' gun, the invention which has made it so much easier to deal with wild animals. This was obviously a case in which it must be used. But it was essential to have a fairly accurate idea of the patient's weight. This was not difficult with small creatures but with the large ones it was possible to be a hundred pounds out on an estimate. A mistake like that could result in either overdosage or underdosage and either would be dangerous. Also, it was important to shoot accurately in order to avoid doing damage to parts of the body where there is no muscle. If, for example, the dart penetrated the abdomen, the animal would die.

Maurice climbed back over the barrier. 'We must be off. The trouble is that I get so absorbed in this place that I almost forget I've got other patients waiting for me.'

Out on the main road, we were making up a little for lost time, when, to my dismay, a Police car suddenly appeared from a side road and waved us down.

'Now what?' I wondered apprehensively as a big Sergeant walked over towards us, but I needn't have worried.

Maurice said, 'Hello, Jim. Dog run over?'

The policeman shook his head. 'Not this time. It's those gippos farther up the road. They've got a pony that doesn't look right to me. It's pretty lame. Will you have a look at it?'

Maurice pulled a face. 'I'll never get rich on the jobs you chaps put in my way. Do I get paid?'

The Sergeant laughed. 'I shouldn't think so. On the other hand, you won't get pinched for speeding.'

Round the bend in the road we came to a bit of waste

and on which stood a few caravans. As we drew up, a sullen looking man came forward.

'Stay in the car,' Maurice muttered, 'better keep an eye on things.'

I saw his point a few minutes later when several very dirty children came up and stood eyeing me curiously.

'Hello,' I said, 'do you live here?' I nodded towards the caravans.

They looked at each other and then back at me but said nothing. Obviously, if you asked silly questions around here you got no answer at all, so I sat still and stared back at them. After a while they began walking round the car and one small boy climbed up to look in the back window. The eldest child pulled the outside mirror round as far as it would go and then reached out for the windscreen wipers.

With a sigh of relief I remembered a tin of sweets we kept in the car. I opened the window and called out, 'Would you like some of these?'

Four pairs of dirty little paws flashed out and, in a few seconds, the tin was empty.

It didn't make much difference. They still hung around, kicking idly at the tyres, until I suddenly thought of turning on the radio. Pop music blared out and the children became alive, jumping and jigging about as though they were at a disco.

Then Maurice appeared from somewhere round the back and the children melted away like shadows, still jerking and swaying like puppets on strings.

As we drove off, I asked curiously, 'What was wrong with the pony?'

'Its back tendons were inflamed. I gave the man something to rub in which should do the trick if they will only rest the animal.'

'Did you get paid?'

'Well, in a way, there's a nice fat rabbit in the boot!'

'Lovely,' I said, 'rabbit pie tomorrow. Now, while we still have a little time, let's talk about our summer holidays.'

'Oh! No!' Maurice gave a groan, 'Well, tell me the worst. What have you planned?'

'If you remember, we decided it would be nice for a change if we took a furnished cottage close to the sea.'

'O.K. We'll have to get a Locum first then we'll see what we can find.'

'No,' I said firmly, 'not this time. This time we'll do things the other way round. Whenever we try to get the Locum first we end up down at your Mother's house in the country because we've been too late to book up anywhere. This year we'll get the cottage first then you'll just have to get someone.'

'That's all very well,' Maurice said in an injured tone, 'you make it sound as though I never try to get anyone.'

I had to admit this was true.

A Vet cannot just close his Surgery and tell the farmers and his other clients that he will be taking a well-earned rest. If he has no partner or assistant, then he must find another Vet to do his work. Sick animals must be attended to or the clients will go elsewhere.

I resolved not to be downcast. 'Never mind, we'll begin studying the advertisements in the *Veterinary Record*. Meantime I'll try and find a cottage.'

'No harm in that,' Maurice turned the car into the bumpy lane leading to Harebell Farm and, in a few minutes, we drew up in the yard.

Mr Miller came across to us from the cowshed. He was one of our favourite farmers. A big, cheerful man with a relaxed manner and a fund of good stories. 'Well, well, nice to see you both. The wife will be pleased too. She's just making a cup of tea.'

As I got out of the car, he said, 'Tell her we'll be along in a minute.'

He and Maurice went off and I made my way towards the farmhouse.

Mrs Miller's kitchen was warm and filled with the mouth-watering smell of newly baked scones. Soon I was sitting at the big table having a good old feminine heart-to-heart. We discussed life in general and our figures in particular.

'I've given up worrying,' said Mrs Miller, 'people expect a farmer's wife to be – well – plump, so why should I disappoint them? Have another scone.'

'I shouldn't,' I said, as I helped myself, 'I'll never be able to get into my swimsuit when we go on holiday.'

'Holiday? What's that?'

Mr Miller and Maurice came through the doorway.

'I hardly know what the word means,' said the farmer, 'it's years since I had one.'

Maurice laughed as he sat down beside me. 'She's trying to pin me down, but, as usual, it all depends on getting a Locum.'

'Locums!' Mr Miller sat down heavily, 'Don't talk to me about them.'

He looked at me. 'Did Maurice tell you about that young man you had last year?'

'No, what happened?'

'There was this cow who wouldn't come "bulling".
That means, come into season,' he explained kindly, for
my benefit, 'so we called in your Locum who gave her an
injection. Still she wouldn't come, so, at the end of the
week, he gave another injection. After that, he told me
she'd better be sent in to the knackers. Good job I didn't
act on his advice. Then Maurice came back from holiday
and immediately examined the cow – as the Locum should
have done – she was well in calf already.'

'Oh! dear!' I said, and hurriedly drank some more tea.
The conversation was not going the right way.

'Never mind,' said Mrs Miller comfortably, 'you must
have your holiday and Locums are a necessary evil. Have
another scone.'

Half-an-hour later, as we drove home, I noticed an
unpleasant though not unfamiliar smell in the car. I
looked suspiciously at Maurice and he grinned.

'Sorry about that. One of the Millers' cows caught me
off guard. She didn't like me putting my arm up her
behind. I'll open the window a bit more.'

He glanced sideways at me. 'The joys of being a Vet's
wife.'

I laughed, 'It's a rich life, even though you don't
exactly reek of money.'

Chapter 4

———◆———

'Pigs,' said Bill Boyd, 'are fascinating creatures. Full of character and very intelligent.'

We were sitting in the farm manager's house having a coffee before doing a tour of the piggery. Bill was a great friend of ours. A burly man in his mid thirties, a cheerful bachelor living alone and managing a small farm owned by a businessman who came down at weekends.

Whenever Maurice was called out to the animals he had to allow plenty of time because Bill took life in a very leisurely fashion. A visit to him was an experience not to be missed, so, when it was possible, I went along as well.

Bill had many interests. Farming, horses, the local girls and the merits of various kinds of beer. But his great passion was pigs. As soon as the subject arose, as it invariably did, his eyes lit up and he was off. Extolling their virtues, praising their exploits and insisting that they were endowed with strong personalities and were all individuals in their own right.

This particular call was for Maurice to castrate some piglets – a job that must be done when they are about eight weeks old.

'I'm just having my coffee,' Bill said, when we arrived, 'come and join me. We'll have a drink afterwards. You'll need it,' he added to Maurice, 'it's Bloody Mary's litter.'

'Oh! Lord!' Maurice grimaced, 'The Vet's nightmare! I'd sooner face an angry gorilla any time.'

'She can be awkward,' Bill admitted, handing round the cups, 'all the same she produces extremely good piglets.'

'Have you got anyone to help you?' I asked anxiously. 'Last time Maurice's trousers were torn to shreds and the cleaner complained about the mess on his jacket.'

Bill threw back his head and roared his appreciation. 'I'll never forget it. I thought I'd got her jammed in a corner behind that bit of wood but, as soon as Maurice went near her piglets, she burst out, knocked me flat and chased Maurice up on to the rafters. Never seen anyone climb so fast.'

'Very funny,' said Maurice, 'I think I'll charge you entertainment tax as well as danger money. What's Bloody Mary like this time?'

'Just as bad. More than we can cope with alone – I've got the cowman to come and give us a hand. He's up in the top field at the moment so we've got plenty of time. Talking of pigs,' he added unnecessarily, 'I've got a bit of a problem with Bella. You remember, I had to bring her up on the bottle – she was so weak she never got a look in at the milk bar with her brothers and sisters shoving her around. I put her in with that lamb that had been rejected by its mother. They became inseparable but last week the lamb was sold and Bella is pining. She keeps breaking out and trying to find her pal. She's a big girl now and it's no joke chasing her around.'

'Keep you fit,' said Maurice hard-heartedly, 'she'll be all right as soon as she gets her first litter. Motherhood will solve that problem.'

We walked down to the piggery which was a magnificent affair with all mod. cons., warm and under cover with an open field at the back where the animals were turned out for exercise.

'It's always so beautifully clean and comfortable,' I said admiringly, and Bill chuckled.

'Naturally,' he said, 'I spend a lot of time here, you know. Often come down at night too, to make sure they're all right. What do you think of my new doors? They've got these sliding shutters so that I can peep through without alarming them.'

'No animals were ever more pampered,' said Maurice, 'you're as big a nut case as Bloody Mary.'

'Well, I've got some of the best pigs in the county,' said Bill proudly, 'and they respond to care and affection. The truth is,' he added mournfully, 'I hate to sell any of them. If this were my own farm, I don't think I ever would.'

Maurice was looking over the wall of a nearby sty. 'Hello, I see Daphne is back.'

'Yes – well,' Bill looked embarrassed, 'that's what I mean. We sold her to old Jim Baker, the farmer next door, but she wouldn't settle. Kept breaking out and coming back here. You could hear her talking away to herself as she came up the drive then she'd just push into her old sty and look at me as if to say, "Aren't you glad to see me?" Old Jim got very fed up so I took her back. Had no option, really.'

He looked at our amused faces and grinned, 'I know, I know. You think I'm off my head. I suppose I am. But pigs can get you that way. Perhaps it would be a good thing if I got married – a wife would soon sort me out. But then, I'd only ask a girl who was keen on pigs and they're few and far between. That's the trouble.'

'Poor old Bill,' said Maurice with feeling, 'you're in a bad way. Never mind, I'll make a few enquiries around my pig farming clients and see if they've got any eligible daughters.'

Bill looked alarmed. 'Don't do that for heaven's sake! I've been out with most of them already. Actually . . .' he hesitated and his tanned cheeks turned slowly red, 'I have met someone. Marvellous girl. But I daren't even tell her I'm a farmer, let alone a pig addict. She works in London and lives in a flat. Very, very smart. Far too good for me.'

We stopped dead and stared at him. 'How did you meet her?' I asked.

'I'll tell you later. Here comes Ted. Better start on Bloody Mary's little boys.'

Ted was as large as Bill, with a big, rosy face. I felt a little less uneasy. Two huge men like that could surely control one angry sow.

With a large wooden door carried in front of them, they entered the sty and, in spite of Bloody Mary's loud protestations, edged her down the little passage and out into the field at the back, thus separating her from her litter.

The piglets immediately went into a panic, squealing hysterically to Mama for help, but they were soon cornered behind the door. Ted leant up against it to keep them in and Bill picked them up, one at a time, letting the gilts back into the sty. Each little boar was handed to Maurice who 'dealt' with it in about fifteen seconds and then put it down on the ground where it joined the others, seemingly oblivious to the fact that its whole life style had been changed.

In view of Ted's ribald comments, I strolled tactfully out of earshot. Then, suddenly, I heard fierce 'barking' and there was Bloody Mary, ears flapping, eyes red with rage, charging towards me. She had burst through from the field and was making for the empty sty beside the one in which her offspring were still squealing blue murder.

I yelled out a warning and dived through the door on the far side of the sty, then watched in horror as she began to clamber over the dividing wall.

Maurice shouted, 'That's the last one,' and, dropping the indignant little boar, he leapt with Ted and Bill to safety.

Only just in time, for Bloody Mary heaved herself over the top and slithered down into the sty, where she stood, still breathing fire and fury, over her young.

I emerged cautiously from my hiding place and Maurice mopped his brow. 'There must be easier ways of earning a living.'

Ted grinned at me and ambled back to his cowshed, whilst Bill chuckled. 'We've earned that drink, come on back to the house.'

As he set out the glasses on the kitchen table, I reminded him, 'You were going to tell us about this girl you've met, Bill. Are you really in love at last?'

He paused in the middle of opening a bottle. 'She'd never have me,' he said gloomily, 'we live totally different lives. She shares a flat with my cousin Dick's girl-friend. I met her at a party Dick threw to celebrate passing his Finals. He's just qualified as a Vet,' he added turning to Maurice, 'you remember him, don't you? He was down here last summer.'

Maurice nodded. 'Keep to the point,' he said, 'what

about this girl?'

'Well, nothing, really,' Bill stared into his glass, 'we got on very well and I took her out once or twice, but she's never been down here. Wouldn't like to ask her.'

'Don't be silly,' I said firmly, 'get your cousin to bring his girl-friend and invite her as well. You'll never know until you ask her. If she loves you, she'll love your work.'

Bill looked at me incredulously, 'You're an optimist, I wish I could believe you. But perhaps I'll have a go. Dick is doing Locums at the moment to gain experience so I'll ask him as soon as he's free.'

'Locums?' I seized on the word and looked at Maurice. 'Did you hear that? How about our holiday?'

'A newly qualified man . . .' Maurice looked doubtful, but Bill said, 'He's pretty good. His father's a Vet so he knows more about General Practice than the average student.'

'Well, O.K., bring him down here and we'll have a chat. I can see I can't get out of taking a holiday,' Maurice smiled at me and I was delighted. Things were working out well.

'Let's hope he's not too booked up,' I said, 'and, Bill, mind you make him bring his girl-friend and her flat mate – what's her name?'

Bill's eyes lit up. 'Mary,' he said reverently.

'Bl – ' Maurice bit back the word and I nearly choked over my drink.

Bill stared at us for a moment, then threw back his head and roared with laughter. 'Do you know, it never occurred to me,' he gasped at last, 'but I assure you there's no resemblance whatever.'

We chuckled all the way home and Maurice said, 'I

can't imagine what his girl-friend is like, but, until we see her, I'm stuck with this awful vision of a raging female with flapping ears and glaring red eyes.'

'You never know,' I replied, 'that may be just what turns Bill on.'

Chapter 5

When you own a dog your life is enriched by years of devotion, friendship and gaiety. The warm companionship of a happy dog, stretched out luxuriantly in front of the fire, feet twitching in a dream of chasing rabbits, the joyous greeting on your return home, the sensitive understanding of your moods, all this unquestioning love is a gift to treasure. And, when you are worrying over the problems of life, a gentle paw placed quietly on your knee is a therapy for many wounds.

But this generous, selfless life is far too short and, sooner or later, you are going to experience that desolate parting that all dog lovers dread. It is the price you pay and it is always better that you should suffer it rather than let your old friend feel unnecessary pain. We have been through that sorrowful ordeal several times and, when our clients have to endure the same unhappiness, we feel the utmost compassion for them. We know the heartache only too well.

Through the years we have had a succession of English springer spaniels, part of our family, adored by the children and devoted to us all. To their master they give perhaps their greatest love. A deep understanding seems to exist between them for which few words are needed. Wherever Maurice is, his dog is never far away. Waiting in his office for him to finish Surgery, out in the car with him on his calls and bounding ahead through the fields and woods in all kinds of weather.

Each of our dogs has had its own individuality and is remembered with stories of its likes and dislikes, its endearing and amusing habits.

There was Major, gentle and very beautiful, with a thick, wavy coat and satiny head, self appointed protector and friend to our little handicapped daughter. He seemed to understand that she was helpless and would sit beside her on the grass while she played with his long, silky ears and snuggled fearlessly against him. Even if, unwittingly, she hurt him a little, he never protested and, if she began to get tired or needed me, he would bark warningly until I arrived.

Then our little boy was born and soon learned to walk. His favourite method was to grasp a handful of Major's coat and pull himself along and his great delight was to be allowed to ride on his friend's back.

When Johnny was about eighteen months old, Stephanie began to die. It was a terrible time and, for three months, we watched her gradually fade away. During that time the whole household revolved round our little daughter and Major got the minimum of attention. He seemed to feel our suffering and became so unobtrusive that we hardly noticed his presence. Often, however, we would find him lying outside Stephanie's bedroom door, pricking his ears at every sound of her voice and, sometimes, giving a soft little whimper.

A year after Stephanie's death, our third child was born and Major seemed to share our joy that we had another little girl and became her slave right away. But, five years later, one sad evening, we were in tears as we looked down at him lying stretched out before the fire. Maurice had just completed his examination and we knew the worst.

'There's nothing I can do for him; it's inoperable, and I can't let him suffer,' Maurice said. 'We must let him go while he's still happy.'

The next day Major went to sleep for the last time in his own bed with his master stroking him and thanking him for all the love he had given us. His tail thumped gently up and down as he closed his eyes and we knew we had done all we could.

We buried him up in the woods where he had spent so many happy hours and, whenever we pass that way, we always pause and think gratefully of the old friend who helped us through so many difficult years.

When our new dog arrived he was cowed and unhappy after a long railway journey. A few months old, he needed all the affection we could give. Margaret fell on him with cries of joy but Johnny hung back. He stroked the puppy once and then went quickly out of the room with tears in his eyes. At ten years old it was not easy to switch allegiance and this new dog was a stranger – almost an interloper.

At tea we tried to think up a name for the new arrival and, after several suggestions, Johnny began to show a little interest. 'What about "Robin"?' he said slowly, 'and "Robbie" for short?'

We looked at the reddish brown coat and bright eyes and decided at once that this was absolutely right. 'Robin he shall be,' said Maurice, 'a grand name.'

Johnny blushed with pleasure but, apart from a quick glance every now and then, he took no further notice of the dog.

Margaret went to bed reluctantly, coming back several

times to assure Robin that she would see him in the morning. When, at last, she had settled down, Johnny said thoughtfully, 'Do you think she's forgotten about Major already?'

'No, and neither have we,' Maurice answered, 'but this dog needs your love too. How would you feel if, without being told anything, you were suddenly taken away from all your family and given to strangers?'

Johnny looked serious. Then he bent down and stroked the puppy who responded by bounding joyously up at him.

'We won't check him yet,' said Maurice, 'he must have a little time to settle in before we begin his training. I'm pretty sure he'll be a fine dog.'

'He'll never be better than Major,' Johnny's voice was sharp with unhappiness.

'If he's only half as good he'll be all right,' said Maurice gently, 'each dog is different so let's wait and see how this one develops.'

We expected a bit of trouble the first night but, after a preliminary whimper or two, Robin settled down in his bed in the kitchen. It wasn't until dawn that he began to wail. We awoke slowly and reluctantly and, as Maurice put on his dressing gown, he said, 'I hope I shan't find too much of a mess!'

He was gone only a few minutes. 'You've been quick. What happened?'

'I wasn't needed.' Maurice shut the door quietly behind him. 'Johnny's down there with everything under control.'

'Did he see you?'

'No. I looked round the door and Robin was lying in his bed with Johnny on his knees beside him. I heard him say "I'm not allowed to take you up to my bed, Robbie, so I'll stay here with you for a while." I think,' he added, with a smile, 'that they will console each other very well.'

Soon Robin became a joy and delight to us all. A complete contrast to his gentle predecessor, he developed into a bold buccaneer, a little more difficult to train but never forgetting a rule once he had accepted its inevitability. He was utterly fearless and guarded us all so tenaciously that, at first, it was almost embarrassing.

We went on holiday and took him on to the beach where he was ordered to be quiet and sit still beside his master. Then I went into the water with the children and began swimming around. Suddenly, Robin could bear it no longer. He plunged in after us and, before I knew what was happening, he had grabbed a mouthful of my swimsuit and pulled me back to safety, much to the amusement of the other folk on the beach. Maurice came down and held him but it was no use. Slipping his collar he plunged in once more and 'rescued' Johnny, looking sideways at Margaret who was playing around in the shallows. It was only when his master came in and swam around with us all that Robin saw the point and joined us, always, however, keeping a weather eye open if we ventured too far away.

Soon he became Maurice's shadow and the relationship between them was so close that they seemed able to read each other's thoughts.

Sitting stroking Robin one day, Maurice said, 'You know, sometimes, when you have had a succession of animals, there comes, if you are lucky enough, the one perfect dog. In my case, this is the one. The best dog I have ever had.'

36

But, five years later, fate dealt us a cruel blow.

Maurice came home one lunchtime in late winter, after having been to a distant farm. As he got out of his car, I saw him suddenly stop and watch the dog who was ahead of him, and I saw then that Robin was walking rather stiffly.

'What's the matter with him?' I asked. 'His legs seem to hurt him.'

'Can't understand it,' Maurice looked concerned and bending down he examined Robin who stood unusually still.

'Nothing that I can see. We've been to old Gooding's farm over at Woodfield. It was cold so I just gave him a quick run over the common. I had two more calls after that and then I came straight home.'

Half-an-hour later Robin had a kind of muscular spasm and I saw Maurice turn white.

'My God!' he said, and then, seeing my alarm, he added, 'I can't be sure but I'm going to get everything ready. It looks as though he's picked up some poison – strychnine, I'm afraid. If so, it's too late to make him sick – it's already in the bloodstream.'

We took him into the Surgery and Maurice said, 'He must be given a general anaesthetic. It's the only treatment that may save him.'

Another spasm and Maurice's fears were justified.

'He must have picked up something on that common land,' Maurice's hand trembled as he got the injection ready. 'There are several poultry farms round there and I expect they're troubled with foxes. Some devil has probably filled a dead chicken with strychnine and left it out in the open for a fox, which has taken it, eaten some and died, leaving the rest. Robin must have found a bit lying around. If I ever find out who did it I'll . . .'

But this was no time for anger. We had to act quickly. Maurice lifted the dog on to the table. 'Come on, old boy. We'll soon make you better,' he said, and held him close for a second. Robin whimpered lovingly and hardly noticed the needle. He quickly went limp and we stood looking at each other.

I felt my eyes fill with tears and Maurice put his arm round me.

'This is why I have to anaesthetise him: the object is to stop the spasms as it is these muscular contractions that kill. They tighten everything up, stopping the breathing and, eventually, the heart muscles contract fatally. For twenty-four hours he must stay under, then I will allow him to come out of the anaesthetic a little, examine his reflexes and put him under again for perhaps another twenty-four hours.'

We put Robin in the kitchen where we could keep watch over him and, that evening, we moved his bed to the fire in the living room and Maurice spent the night beside him, turning him over at regular intervals.

Next day, when he tested the reflexes, the spasms returned, so he was given the second dose of anaesthetic.

Our feelings during that time alternated between hope and fear. Our children, by now teenagers, had such faith in their father that they did not doubt everything would be all right and we tried to keep optimistic for their sake.

The next morning Robin showed signs of coming round and, this time, there were no more spasms. Our spirits lifted and we began to hope that, at last, he would survive. But, suddenly, as Maurice and I were watching, his breathing became laboured. We lifted him quickly but his tongue turned blue and, in a few seconds, our lovely Robin was dead.

It was 'cold' pneumonia. A lot of mucus had suddenly formed in the lungs causing death, literally, by drowning.

We have never mourned a dog so much. This brutal end to a young life was almost too much to bear and, for our children, it was the greatest tragedy they had ever experienced.

During those sad days, Maurice was called out to the farm he had visited near the common where Robin had picked up the poison and, this time, it was the farmer's dog suffering from the same symptoms.

He received the same treatment and two days later he recovered. Maurice remarked bitterly, 'I saved *his* dog yet I couldn't save my own.'

The Police were told, enquiries were made but no one ever found the culprit.

There was only one thing to do, although we had little heart for it. We drove up to the Midlands to see the man from whom we had bought Robin. He bred springer spaniels and was a great authority on training them as gun dogs. Full of sympathy, he took us outside to see the inmates of his kennels.

'I have one in mind for you, a dog full of character, a year old and a nephew of your Robin.'

On the way, we passed an enclosure and suddenly Margaret stopped dead. 'Look!' she pointed. 'That's the one I want. He's just like Robin.'

The spaniel came up to the wire and nuzzled her hand. We stared unbelievingly – Robin's double.

But our friend shook his head. 'No, Margaret,' he said

gently, 'don't have him, my dear. He's nine years old and he's not your Robin. Look into his eyes.'

She did as he said, then, turning away, she burst into tears. 'I would love to have him,' she sobbed, 'but you're right. He's not our Robin.'

The new dog had the appalling name of Fang and he was nothing like Robin but we knew when we saw him that he would soon have his place in our hearts.

The journey back was a nightmare. At frequent and regular intervals Fang was sick. He seemed quite untroubled about it calmly throwing up then settling down again with a deep sigh of relief.

Cleaned, fed and installed in a new bed, Fang sat and surveyed his new family. The bed was his first real taste of comfort as hitherto he had slept in an outside kennel with his brothers. He kept coming out and quickly jumping back again. He stretched out, rolled over and made little noises of pleasure as though he simply couldn't believe such comfort existed.

We discussed his name but it was difficult to think of anything but Robin until, at last, we decided to call him Robert.

And Robert, lovely Robert, has become another faithful friend with funny, endearing ways and a great, loving heart. As with our other dogs, Maurice is his god and they are inseparable.

I sometimes think that, if and when, we ever get to heaven's gates, all Maurice's dogs will be there waiting to greet him. If, however, there is a notice outside, saying, 'No dogs allowed here,' then I foresee trouble. Maurice will probably refuse to enter. Eternity without a dog beside him is not his idea of heaven.

Chapter 6

———————◆———————

It was going to be a difficult day, I could tell that from the start when Maurice was called out to a calving case at 5 a.m.

Breakfast was late, the Waiting Room was crammed with a variety of patients for morning Surgery and the telephone rang incessantly, piling up the calls. It was also our Wedding Anniversary.

Fate always seems to play tricks on us when we plan to go out in the evening. When I think back to the number of cancelled tables at local hotels or the times when we have arrived much later than arranged, I wonder that we still have the audacity even to contemplate going out at all.

'You'll have to do your dragon act on the telephone today,' said Maurice as he set off on his calls, 'put people off till tomorrow if at all possible.'

He grinned at my worried expression, 'Cheer up! We'll make it this time whatever happens.'

Almost as soon as his car had disappeared, the telephone rang again.

'My budgie's beak needs clipping and I'd like it done today.'

I explained that Maurice was so busy that he couldn't fit any more calls in and that he would be along tomorrow and chalked that one up to me.

'My Freddy is no better,' said the next caller in an accusing voice, 'Mr Bowring gave me some tablets and said he would be all right when they were finished but he isn't well yet.'

'Haven't you any tablets left?' I asked. I knew this client of old.

'Oh! Yes. Plenty — well — nearly all in fact. Freddy just won't take them. I don't think he has any faith in them. Mr Bowring gave him the first one but it didn't do any good so when I offer them to him he just turns away in disgust.'

I did my best to penetrate that foggy mind and told her various ways in which she could fool her Freddy but I knew it was no use. This was one of those cases where the dog ruled its owner, so I told her to bring it along to the Surgery tomorrow and hurriedly rang off.

I was in the middle of ironing when the next call came. This time it was the Zoo. One of the monkeys in quarantine was off colour — could I get my husband there as soon as possible.

I looked at the list of places he had given me and rang the first one. He had just left, they told me and, when I rang the next number, the woman who answered was so deaf that I was not able to pass on the message. I managed to make her understand that I wanted him to ring his home and hoped she wouldn't forget.

Ten minutes later I had just decided I had better ring another place when the telephone rang again.

'Oh! Hello, darling,' I said quickly, 'they want you at the Zoo.'

'Do they now?' said a strange voice, 'I knew I was a bit eccentric but . . .'

Filled with confusion I apologised and found I was talking to the local Vicar who wanted Maurice to call and see his cat.

After that, I decided I needed a coffee and was about to sit down when Maurice came through.

Sipping my drink in unaccustomed peace, I eyed the telephone malevolently. I couldn't really hate it, of course. It was vital to us and we should get extremely depressed if it never rang, but how nice it must have been before it was invented.

A Vet's life was very different then and a Vet's wife must have had a whale of a time. She would see her husband off in his pony-trap and all messages that came to the door would be dealt with by one of the servants. There wouldn't be many servants though, because a Vet's social position was not very high up the ladder. He was the horse doctor who also knew a bit about cattle and pigs and practically nothing about small animals. The horse population was enormous with all the tradesmen keeping stables, the breweries with their heavy draught horses, the timber merchants, the doctors and professional folk with their carriages and pairs, and a constant stream of horse-drawn traffic all needing attention.

Not so good for the dogs and cats in those days. Come to that, it wasn't all that wonderful for the horses and cattle either. With no antibiotics, no steroids and all the nostrums and quackeries that surrounded medicine, animals must have had a hard job to survive.

The telephone brought me back to earth again. An enquiry about spaying a bitch. I gave the usual information – bring it in to the morning Surgery, nothing to eat or drink beforehand and they could pick it up that evening – and, when I put down the receiver, I wondered what the old horse doctors would have thought of that.

Evening Surgery was a bit rushed but I managed to get away early and went upstairs to dress. It looked as if we were actually going to be on time and I prepared to enjoy myself.

I heard the telephone ring when I was in the bathroom and, by the time I returned to the bedroom, Maurice was there.

'Hurry up,' I said, 'you've only got a quarter of an hour.'

Then I saw his face.

'Oh! No! What was that last call, then?'

'A horse with colic out at Hobden's stables,' said Maurice, 'I'll be as quick as I can but it may be a long job.'

He waited for me to explode – and I did. After I'd expressed my opinion of the Veterinary profession in a few well chosen words, I calmed down.

'Oh! Well,' I said resignedly, 'I'll ring up the hotel and cancel the table.'

'Just tell them we'll be a bit late. I'll make it somehow.'

I regretted my outburst as soon as he had left and began to worry that he would drive too fast and have an accident, so when the telephone rang again I was expecting the worst.

'I'm just leaving the stables,' he said cheerfully, 'it wasn't too bad. Be home in twenty minutes.'

We enjoyed our dinner immensely and when we were drinking our coffee Maurice remarked, 'See that couple over there? He's a client of mine. A very rich businessman. He and his wife come here regularly. It was he who recommended this place to me. Don't they look bored?'

I half turned and saw a fat bald man with a tight mouth

and a very smart woman with a face like vinegar. 'Goodness! What a miserable looking couple.'

Maurice grinned, 'That's what a regular life does for you. This is no treat to them. Wouldn't you rather be a Vet's wife in spite of what you said earlier on this evening?'

'Not just any Vet's wife, it's got to be you.'

That night the telephone rang again. As I switched on the bedside lamp I saw it was 2 a.m.

'That horse again,' said Maurice, pulling on his clothes, 'I'll have to give it another injection.'

It was pouring with rain and, as I heard the car drive away, I thought once more of the Vets of the past. The trap to be dragged out into the yard, the pony led out of the stable, harnessed and backed into the shafts, the candle lamps to be lit and then the slow drive through dark lanes, exposed to all weathers. Thank goodness for a closed, heated car. There was something to be said for modern times after all.

Modern methods save many lives but patients need devoted nursing too and, sometimes, the one is as essential as the other. This was brought home to me when, one evening, Maurice came into the kitchen carrying a dog basket and set it down beside the boiler.

He adjusted the blanket round the little bundle inside and said he was worried about the pup. Earlier that evening he had taken two marbles out of the little dog but it was no straightforward operation. The owners had only brought him into the Surgery after he had been sick for five days. Consequently he was very weak and in bad shape for a general anaesthetic.

Going to the basket, I took another look at him. A little sandy fellow with a snowy white chest and two white

45

forelegs. He belonged to a little girl in the village who had herself only just come out of hospital after a big operation on a crippled leg.

'Gillian adores Sandy,' said Maurice, 'if anything happens to him . . .' he frowned. 'Well, I must do what I can.'

We were finishing our meal when Sandy began to whimper and Maurice went swiftly over to him. 'That's the sound I want to hear.' He rubbed the dog's back vigorously and the whining ceased. He lifted an eyelid and gently touched the eye-ball. 'All the same, he's still very deeply under and there's not much eye reflex yet.'

I began washing up.

'How long do you think it will be before he comes round?'

'Hard to say. I gave him a short-acting anaesthetic. He should be well on his way in a couple of hours. If there are no reflexes back in that time I shall be getting worried.'

He paused, 'Oh! Lord! There's the phone. Hope it's nothing urgent.'

Alone in the kitchen I knelt and stroked the little dog. There is something so pathetic about an unconscious animal. I thought of the little girl who lay waiting and longing for her pet and I called 'Sandy, Sandy,' hoping he would hear me through the swirling mists of oblivion.

When Maurice came back he said, 'That was Mr Forbes. Wanted to know what he could tell Gillian. The poor child is worrying herself sick. I told him to say that Sandy is fast asleep and dreaming of chasing rabbits.'

He sat down and took up the evening paper. 'You go and watch television or something. I'm going to stay here.'

I shook my head. 'I'd rather be with you. Let's just hope there won't be any calls.'

As if in answer, the telephone rang again.

This time when Maurice returned he picked up his case. 'Hillside Farm,' he said. 'Cow with milk fever. I'll be as quick as I can.'

He had been gone about an hour when, suddenly, a queer little sound came from the dog basket and I went over to investigate.

Sandy was going to be sick. I grabbed the newspaper just in time. When it was over, he lay spent and exhausted. His breathing was very shallow and his heartbeats faint. This collapse was serious and, for a moment, I wondered what best to do. I was preparing a heart stimulant injection when Maurice came through the door.

A few seconds later he said, 'He's responding. I'll give him an intravenous glucose saline in a quarter of an hour. I'm afraid it's touch and go, now.'

The injection given, he adjusted the speed on the drip and strapped the tube on to the leg. 'That will take about an hour, let's have some coffee while we're waiting.'

It was getting late when I heard him say, 'Look!' and, taking one of Sandy's forepaws, he stretched out the leg and gently pinched a toe. There was a little movement as the dog tried to pull it back.

'You can go up to bed now, I'll just stay here a little longer.'

Some time later the shrilling of the telephone woke me from sleep and I switched on the light to see the time. Three o'clock and still Maurice had not come up to bed. I pulled on my dressing gown and went downstairs.

He was replacing the receiver. 'Nothing urgent,' he

said, 'I've given them some advice. Come and see Sandy.'

The little dog lying there looked very different from the poor limp creature I had last seen. His breathing was deep and strong and, as I stroked his back, I could feel life pulsing through him.

'Sandy!' I called, 'Sandy!'

He lifted his head slightly, and suddenly two sleepy little eyes were looking straight at me. Then he sighed contentedly and snuggled down again.

Maurice said, 'He'll have a long sleep and, tomorrow, he'll be full of beans.'

'Tomorrow . . .? It's tomorrow now!'

He looked at the clock. 'So it is. Well, never mind. It's been worth it. I think the saline drip saved him.'

'Modern methods are wonderful,' I said, 'and so are modern Vets.'

My husband smiled, 'I'd like that in writing, it will come in useful next time I'm late for a party.'

Chapter 7

———◆———

I was still worried about our holiday. After that talk with Bill Boyd and the mention of his newly qualified cousin, nothing more had been said. So when Bill rang to say he had a sow which had recently farrowed but was off her food, I decided to have a word with him when I went along with Maurice. It has long been my opinion that if you want a thing badly enough you have to do all the organising yourself. At least you have to start the ball rolling otherwise it stays there and everybody steps over it. We had the chance of a Locum, a good one too, from all accounts, and we needed a holiday. I certainly did and although Maurice invariably protested that the best thing about a holiday was the day you returned home, he was always refreshed after a few weeks away from disturbed nights and the tyranny of the telephone.

We went out to the car and Maurice looked in his appointment book. 'A mixed bag today, starting with a goldfish.'

He grinned at my incredulous stare. 'Well, two goldfish, to be exact. This Miss Downes rang while you were getting ready. I can't imagine what the trouble can be, but she hinted at something rather indelicate.'

Intrigued, I watched when we pulled up in front of a neat semi-detached house and, when the door opened, I caught a glimpse of a tall, thin woman with greying hair and an anxious expression. She led him in, after shooting me a suspicious glance, and shut the door. Ten minutes later, Maurice emerged and this time the door was slammed behind him.

He put his case on the back seat of the car and settled himself behind the driving wheel. His face was dead-pan and I saw the reason when I noticed the front window curtain move slightly. Then, as we drove away, he began to chuckle.

'Don't keep me in suspense, what was the indelicate problem?'

'*She's* the problem,' Maurice explained. 'She took me into her sitting room and showed me a bowl with these two goldfish swimming round and round, pointed to one of them and said, "I want you to tell me if you think she's – er – if she's going to have – er – well – is she pregnant?" I tried to keep a straight face and told her that no goldfish would ever breed in a bowl but she said . . . ' Maurice became nearly incoherent, 'Listen to this bit – she said "Oh! But I always give them a swim in the bath every day!" '

When I had finished laughing, I asked, 'Did you tell her about putting them in a pond if she wants them to breed?'

'I tried but, of course, it's never any use with people like that. She had this fixed idea that a good swim in the bath was equal to a stroll down Lovers' Lane and that, one day, there would be lots of little baby goldfish as a result. She said she didn't think I was much of a Vet if I couldn't tell her whether or not the female was pregnant. I said I didn't even know if they were male or female and that seemed to finish her. She showed me the door! Bang goes my reputation in that road!'

I asked my usual question, 'Did she pay you for your visit?'

'Oh! No!' Maurice chuckled again, 'No question of that. We parted on fighting terms. Now we're going to see another woman who lives alone but this one is a very different proposition. She lives in a wood with a guard dog and four cats. Nothing whimsical about her. Mrs Hardy is her name and she lives up to it.'

We pulled up in a lane by a gap in the trees. 'This way,' Maurice pointed to a mossy track and we picked our path through bluebells and clumps of primroses. After a few minutes I stopped and drew a deep breath.

'It's heavenly,' I said, 'the lovely smell of an English wood in springtime and – listen – there's the cuckoo.'

We walked on in silence, absorbing all the beauty round us until we came to a clearing where there was a small cottage. A woman with grey, curly hair and a face the colour of a walnut, leant against the doorpost watching our approach.

Four cats were grouped around her, wild looking creatures who arched their backs and rose slowly to their feet. Suddenly, a large Alsatian dog came dashing towards us, growling and barking ferociously. I drew back in alarm but with a shout from the woman he slithered to a halt and went straight back, sitting in front of her, obviously prepared to tear us to pieces at the slightest provocation.

Maurice introduced me and, keeping a respectful distance from the Alsatian, I said, 'That's a fine dog you've got there.'

'Best friend I've ever had,' said Mrs Hardy. Then with a smile and a mischievous glint in her eyes she added,

'He's called George, after my husband. He used to growl like that.'

I was a bit taken aback but Maurice smiled appreciatively. 'Did he obey you instantly like this fellow here?'

Mrs Hardy shook her head, her eyes alight with laughter. 'No. It was the other way round, I'm afraid.' She saw my puzzled look and said, 'Past history, my dear. But I'm a happy woman now.'

She pointed to a large, black tom-cat. 'That's the one with the abscess.'

Maurice bent down to pick him up but, instantly, he and his companions scattered and raced up the nearest trees. To my surprise, Mrs Hardy darted indoors but, a moment later she reappeared, carrying an ancient air rifle.

'Get 'em back in a second,' she muttered as she loaded up, then she aimed at the trunk of one of the trees and fired. There was a rush and the cats scrambled down and tore back to her, purring and rubbing themselves against her legs. Picking up the tom she held him whilst Maurice did his examination and then gave him an injection.

'Now,' she said, 'how about a quick cup of coffee?'

Filled with curiosity about this self-reliant woman, I went into the cottage. It was crowded with furniture, there were books everywhere and great bowls of wild flowers brightened up the dark corners. I sat down in a battered armchair and stroked George who installed himself beside me looking quite different from the fierce watch dog who had greeted us.

'Tell me,' I said, 'why do the cats come back so quickly when you fire that rifle?'

Mrs Hardy gave her attractive smile, 'Well, you see,

they developed this habit of rushing up into the trees when anyone came and I was finding it difficult to get them in at night so, one day, I fired vaguely in their direction, hoping it would frighten them down. Unfortunately, I accidentally hit one and it came tearing down like a tornado. No real harm done, of course, because there's not much power in this old rifle but it must have stung a bit. Somehow, the other cats have cottoned on and now, whenever I want them, I just fire a shot and they come in from all directions.'

We finished our coffee, Maurice gave Mrs Hardy some tablets for the tom and we got up to leave.

'Nice to have met you,' said Mrs Hardy, smiling at me, 'you must come again.'

'I'd love to,' I said truthfully, 'I suppose you feel a bit lonely out here, don't you?'

'Bless you, no,' Mrs Hardy pointed round the room, 'I've got my books and my radio, a bicycle to take me to the village when I need supplies and George to guard me. What more could anyone want? I couldn't bear to live with traffic and noise, to say nothing of next-door neighbours.'

She waved gaily to us as we went back through the wood and Maurice said, 'Quite a character, isn't she?'

I nodded, 'I wonder what her husband was like.'

'George, who growled like an Alsatian?' Maurice smiled, 'I think, from what she has let fall from time to time, that he was a surly brute. I'm sure she prefers having the dog and it probably gives her a lot of satisfaction to shout at him and get instant obedience.'

As we reached the car he looked at his watch. 'We've spent a lot of time on two not exactly lucrative calls. No dilly-dallying at the next place – Marsh Farm.'

'That's the man whose hobby is photography, isn't it? Last time we were there he promised to show me some of his prize winning exhibits.'

'Look, we mustn't waste time. I've got half-a-dozen pregnancy diagnoses to make there and I want to get away as soon as I've finished.'

As we pulled up in the farmyard, Mr Lovell came to meet us. He and his wife were a cheerful couple although they led an extremely hard life. They shared the milking of about forty cows, did the mucking out and worked in the fields. The only help they had was from their three children after school hours and an occasional student in vacation time.

Mr Lovell opened the car door for me. 'Come to see those exhibits I had in the local photographic show? I won a First and a Third.'

'Congratulations,' I said, 'I'd love to see them but I'm afraid we haven't got much time today.'

'Jean's in the kitchen. You go in and she'll show them to you.'

I glanced at Maurice who nodded. 'You've got about half-an-hour, but don't keep me waiting, will you?'

Mr Lovell added teasingly, 'You Vets don't know what work is! Gossiping with the farmers, sipping sherry with old ladies – a wonderful life. I'd change places with you any day.'

They argued amiably as Maurice got ready for the job, stripping off his jacket and rolling up his shirt sleeves. He pulled on his obstetric gown, a large rubber affair with two holes for his arms. He tied the tapes at the back of his neck and then bent down to wash and soap his arms in the pail of warm water standing by the cowshed door.

'Right,' he said, 'now let's join the ladies.'

As they went in to the waiting cows, standing tethered in their stalls, I wandered off towards the farmhouse, stopping on the way to caress and talk to some of the many kittens and cats of all colours and sizes that were a feature of Mr Lovell's farm.

Jean Lovell was ironing at the kitchen table with a huge pile waiting to be done but she stopped when I went in and waved aside my apology for interrupting her.

'Only too pleased to have an excuse for a break, I hate this sort of work – far rather be outside with the animals. Still, it's got to be done so I rush through it somehow. Let's have a coffee.'

'Well, I've already had one,' I said, 'but I can always do with another. Maurice says that as soon as people see me they get out the coffee pot.'

I stroked the large purring tabby cat curled up beside the stove. 'It's a cat's paradise here. How many have you got?'

Mrs Lovell laughed. 'We don't really know. They're Jim's "models" for his photography. Would you like to see his winning entries in the exhibition?'

They were absolutely lovely. Studies of kittens taken in the most adorable attitudes, among the daffodils, climbing on beams, playing with each other, irresistible to even the most confirmed cat haters.

'How does he get them to do things like that?' I asked, pointing to a study of a kitten sitting on a branch and examining its paw with its head on one side.

'Fish paste,' Mrs Lovell laughed as she poured out the

coffee, 'a dab here and a dab there and they hunt around till they find it.'

'Another illusion gone,' I said, helping myself to a biscuit, 'it all boils down to greed. We're all the same.'

Soon it was time for me to leave Mrs Lovell to her ironing and return to the cowshed. Thankfully I saw that Maurice was still working.

'Only one more to do,' he said, and I watched as he put his arm right up the rectum of a large Friesian cow. As he was feeling around for the uterus, she suddenly arched her back and began to strain, tightening up on his arm and making it impossible for him to move his fingers.

'Hold on,' Mr Lovell saw his difficulty, 'I'll soon stop that little game.'

He gave her a good pinch in the lumbar region and, immediately, the cow straightened her back, to Maurice's obvious relief.

'It's O.K.,' he said, 'I can feel the membranes now. She's pregnant all right.' He paused, then added, 'Ten weeks.'

He withdrew his dung-covered arm, plunged it into the bucket and began soaping vigorously.

'That makes five out of six,' he said, 'you'll have to get that first one served again when she comes into season.'

A few minutes later we were on our way to Bill Boyd's farm and, as we approached the drive, Maurice said, 'It won't take long to give that sow an injection but we'll have to forego our usual leisurely chat. I've got to look in at the Zoo to see that ostrich with a growth in its eye. I must be there on time as I've arranged for four keepers to hold it under control.'

'That's going to be difficult, isn't it?' I asked.

'It certainly is. Dangerous things, ostriches. I want to get a piece of the growth to send off to the laboratory. It may take a while, because I must put a local anaesthetic into the eye, wait three or four minutes for it to work then cut a bit out and, during that time, we've got to keep her still.'

He gave me a sideways glance, 'I haven't forgotten about the Locum, so don't worry. I'll ask Bill but we mustn't go into the house or we'll never get away.'

Bill was down at the piggery, looking worried.

'It's Maudie,' he said, 'magnificent litter — fourteen — but she won't eat and she's beginning to lose her milk.'

Maurice grinned at him. 'You look as though your world has collapsed around you. Honestly, Bill, this happens so often and you know I can always put it right.'

He opened his case and took out a syringe. Then he glanced at the sow. 'She's lying on her tummy so that the piglets can't get at her. Sure sign she's losing her milk. Well, let's go to it.'

Bill picked up one end of a large board and handed the other to Maurice. 'She's usually quite good tempered but we'd better not take any chances.'

She began to protest loudly as soon as they entered the sty but they gradually edged her into a corner and I saw Maurice grab hold of one of her ears. Then he put the injection of pituitrin into the thin skin lying behind the ear, the only place on a pig where a fine needle can be used.

He looked down at the squealing piglets. 'Milk bar will be open in thirty seconds flat.'

Bill cheered up instantaneously, watching proudly as

Maudie settled down on her side and the piglets rushed in, pushing and shoving like a crowd in a pub on a Bank Holiday.

'Makes me quite thirsty,' he said, 'come into the house and have a quick one with me.'

Maurice shook his head firmly. 'Sorry, Bill, not today. No time. But one question: What news of your cousin – the Vet?'

'He's coming down on Sunday,' said Bill, 'if you care to come over and have a drink you can talk over your Locum problem.'

He turned to me, 'He's bringing his girl-friend and Mary is coming too. I've taken your advice but I expect it will finish her when she sees how I live.'

'Have you told her you're a farmer, yet?' I asked, and he nodded, 'I warned her on the phone. But I'm only a farm manager and she is – well – you'll see for yourself on Sunday.'

He waved us off, looking disconsolate again and Maurice said, 'Poor old Bill! He's got it badly. Even his pigs don't seem able to comfort him. It'll be interesting to see what this girl is really like. Now, let's get to the Zoo.'

Four men, including the Superintendent, were waiting for us outside the ostriches' sleeping quarters – a large shed at the end of their enclosure.

'We've kept her in,' said George, 'and we've moved the male into a temporary paddock in case he starts getting obstreperous but it's going to be a bit tricky all the same.'

Maurice turned to me. 'You can help here. When we've got the bird under control I'll want my syringe, forceps, scissors and a bottle of formalin for the specimens. If you can hand those to me, I can go in and help hold her down. We must be very quick to avoid getting badly kicked or torn open by those great big toe-nails.'

He opened his case and prepared the syringe, handed me the instruments and I stood at the ready behind him as George pulled back the door of the shed. I saw the ostrich standing at the far end and, even from that distance I noticed that her right eye was half closed. She was moving her head from side to side and, as she stepped forward I caught a glimpse of her main defensive weapons, the two big toes on each foot, with enormous claw-like nails.

'O.K.,' said George. 'One, two, three, go!' and the five men rushed in, grabbing the unfortunate bird and holding on grimly until she was forced down into a crouching position with her legs out in front. To my surprise, although she struggled wildly at first, she made no sound at all and stayed reasonably still when she realised that she had lost the battle.

Holding her neck tightly to keep her immobile, Maurice stretched out his right hand.

'Syringe,' he said.

I went up as close to him as necessary and George comforted me, 'It's O.K., Mrs Bowring, we won't let go if we can help it.'

I watched as Maurice gently pulled her eyelid up and then I saw the cluster of little tumours. Carefully he let fall about half-a-dozen drops into the eye and handed me back the syringe.

'We'll have to give it four or five minutes to work,' he said, 'so keep holding.'

He looked searchingly at the eye. 'It's developed a lot since I saw it last week, the outlook isn't too good. If the lab. confirms that it's malignant I don't think I ought to try to operate. It's not fair on the bird to put her through unnecessary suffering for what is probably a hopeless case. If it's not malign I'll have a go but she may very well die from shock anyway.'

He touched the eye gently. 'Still a bit of reflex action, better wait another minute or two. Now, I want my hands free so will you take over her neck, George?'

George obliged, and took a close look at the eye. 'It's a shame, she's only three years old, just coming on to lay. Not that we've ever had a baby ostrich hatched out here but we're always hoping.'

Maurice touched the eye again. 'I'll go ahead now, may I have the forceps?'

I watched, fascinated, as he pulled down the eyelid; then, taking hold of the growth with the forceps, he took the scissors from me and cut off three small pieces about the size of sweet pea seeds and dropped them into the formalin bottle.

I backed out quickly as the men relaxed their hold on the bird but there was no need to hurry, for she took her time in getting up, shook out her ruffled feathers and stalked indignantly out into the paddock.

'I'll send this off to the lab. today,' said Maurice, as we walked back to the car with George, 'it will be four or five days before we know the answer.'

I was curious to know one thing. 'Why didn't you "dart" her? Surely it would have been easier?'

Maurice shook his head. 'Birds are very unpredictable with anaesthetics, and this only needed a local. We only dart if we can't restrain by any other means.'

We arrived home in time for a late lunch and, as I

whipped up an omelette, I asked Maurice what his afternoon plans were.

'I've got to see a horse at Wood Lane Stables. You can get me there, and then there are some dog and cat jobs in the town. I'll give you the addresses before I leave.'

The afternoon went by in a flash with, happily, no interruptions and, by the time John and Margaret arrived home from school, Maurice was able to join us for tea. He was telling them about the goldfish and Mrs Hardy's way of calling in her cats when their laughter was interrupted by the sound of the telephone.

A few minutes later he came back, frowning. 'Remember that couple I pointed out to you when we were having dinner on our Wedding Anniversary?'

I nodded. 'Rich and bored,' I said.

'Yes. Well, she – Mrs Craig – rang to ask me to call round now and give her poodle his booster injection. It must be now because they're off to Stockholm early tomorrow morning and the dog has to go into kennels this evening.'

'She could have rung earlier,' I said indignantly.

'That's what I told her,' Maurice's frown deepened. 'In fact I told her it wasn't convenient and that, if she wants it done, she must bring it here. I don't mind doing it before evening Surgery but I'm damned if I'm going to turn out again when I've already passed her house twice today. She didn't like it much – she's not used to being thwarted – but I left it at that.'

Twenty minutes later a sharp ring at the door announced her arrival and, as I led her over to the Surgery, she said, 'This is most annoying. I much prefer to have Mr Bowring come to my house.'

'If you had rung earlier,' I replied smoothly, 'he would, of course, have done so but it wasn't convenient for him to go out again just before evening Surgery.'

Her mouth tightened but she said nothing.

I opened the Surgery door and Maurice took the little dog and stood him on the table.

Mrs Craig said, 'Apart from the booster injection I'd like you to give Pierre a thorough examination to make sure he's fit before he goes into kennels. Then, if there is anything wrong with him when we fetch him we can complain.'

I avoided looking at Maurice and concentrated on holding Pierre who was doing his best to bite me. Then, as the needle went in, he gave a little yelp.

Mrs Craig complained, 'Really, Mr Bowring. I think you might be a little more gentle. Pierre is so much more sensitive than the average poodle. He's very highly bred.'

Maurice looked across at me. 'I shan't need you to hold him while I do the examination.' I took the hint and drew Mrs Craig away from the table and tried to make light conversation.

'So you're off to Stockholm tomorrow, how lovely for you. Do you go abroad much?'

She glanced at me indifferently, 'Oh, yes. My husband has business connections in most countries and I nearly always go with him. Not that I enjoy it particularly; after all, one hotel is much like another and shops seem all the same nowadays.'

She turned back to Maurice and watched him in silence until he put Pierre down on the floor.

'He's perfectly O.K.,' he said, 'apart from the fact that

he's rather too fat. He needs plenty of exercise and less food.'

Mrs Craig gathered up the yapping little dog. 'I think I know what's best for Pierre. Now, please send in your bill as soon as possible and don't charge me too much. I often wonder if these booster injections are really necessary. What are they for, anyway?'

'A booster injection,' said Maurice slowly and evenly, 'is a combined vaccine against Hard Pad, Distemper, Virus hepatitis, Leptospiral canicola and Leptospiral icterohaemorrhagica.'

'Oh!' Mrs Craig looked slightly taken aback. She opened her mouth to say something but Maurice's cold stare must have deterred her for she suddenly turned red and made a hurried exit.

Maurice shut the door behind her. 'Bitch!' he said briefly, and went to the sink to wash out his syringe.

I drew a long breath. 'I've seen some odd characters today, but she tops the bill.'

'I'll see that she does,' said Maurice grimly, 'we'll double her account and take it off Mrs Hardy's.'

Chapter 8

Maurice has no Surgeries on Sunday so, as John and Margaret were having some school friends in, we left them in charge of the telephone with instructions to put through only urgent calls and set off for Bill Boyd's farm.

'Will Mr Parker, Bill's boss, be there?' I asked, as we got into the car, 'he usually comes down at the weekends, doesn't he?'

'Not this Sunday,' said Maurice, 'he's in France. I expect that's why Bill has picked today. He's very conscious of not being his own boss since he's met this girl. You know, I still can't get the vision of Bloody Mary out of my mind. I do hope there's no resemblance.'

I laughed. 'Don't be absurd. I'll bet she's one of these model types – you know – beautifully made-up, slim and elegant.'

With a sigh I pulled at my rather tight skirt.

Maurice put his hand on my knee. 'Now, don't you start feeling all inferior, no one can come within an inch of you, so remember that.'

A remark like that is guaranteed to please any wife so, feeling considerably cheered, I prepared to face the gorgeous creature who had captivated Bill.

When we arrived, he was entertaining his guests on the large lawn at the back of the farmhouse. His cousin, a pleasant looking young man, attached himself to Maurice almost immediately and I looked around for someone dressed like a picture out of *Vogue*. A pretty girl in jeans and sweater came up and Bill introduced her as his cousin's girl-friend.

'Actually, they've just got engaged,' he added.

'Congratulations,' I said, 'so you're going to be a Vet's wife. Brave girl!'

She laughed, 'I'm hoping you'll be able to give me a few tips.'

'Is Dick going into general practice?' I asked, 'or is he going to settle for a nice, steady job in the Ministry of Agriculture?'

'He wants to be a country Vet. It sounds lovely to me.'

'Well,' I smiled, 'it's pretty hectic at times but we wouldn't change places with anyone. Are you a good cook?'

'Well, no,' she looked a bit startled, 'I suppose I ought to take lessons. I can only just get by at present.'

'That's good. If you were the Cordon Bleu type, being married to a Vet would probably break your heart. As it is, all you really need to know is how to keep meals hot for long periods and how to dish up something appetising in five minutes flat.'

She looked at me a bit doubtfully for a moment then broke into a delightful smile. 'You've given me confidence, I can see I'm not going to have to be a super housewife and that suits me down to the ground. I'd far rather be out on a horse.'

'That'll be fine, so long as you have a telephone attached to the saddle. That is more important to a Vet's wife than a vacuum cleaner.'

'Don't pay any attention to my wife's horror stories,' Maurice had come up and was standing listening, 'if Dick takes my advice he will get a few years' experience in

65

one of these highly efficient practices where they have all mod. cons. and regular time off. It's only when you are on your own that things get a bit chaotic.'

She giggled attractively and we were still talking when Bill approached carrying a bottle which he proceeded to empty into our glasses.

When Jane had gone off to join her fiancé I looked at Bill. 'Well, where is she? Your Mary, I mean. Don't tell me she couldn't come.'

'You'll never believe this,' he said, and there was a dazed look in his eyes, 'she's down at the piggery. I took them all down there when they first arrived because I was nervous of Mary's reactions and I thought it would be a good way of getting relaxed. To my utter astonishment I couldn't tear her away. She said she'd come up as soon as you came but she hasn't – ah!' – he gazed over my shoulder, 'here she is at last.'

Drifting across the grass came the gorgeous creature, dressed as casually as her friend yet managing to look every bit as seductive as though she were showing off the latest Parisian creation.

Full of apologies she said, 'I'm so sorry I wasn't here when you arrived but I lost all sense of time down there. It made me so homesick. My father is a farmer down in Somerset and he has a thing about pigs. He keeps Large Whites too but I must admit that they're not as fine as these I've just been examining.'

I stared at Bill but he was looking at Mary as though he'd seen a vision of Paradise.

At last he found his voice. 'You – you – never told me,' he stammered and then went bright red as she gave him a dazzling smile

'You never asked me anything about myself.' Then, her beautiful eyes bright with enthusiasm, she added, 'I must tell you about this pig we had. Her name was Myrtle and one day she broke out . . .'

I looked from one to the other, saw that they didn't even know I was there and tactfully faded away.

'Talk about a marriage of true minds,' said Maurice as we drove home, 'and a more unromantic link than pigs I can hardly imagine. By the way,' he added, 'Dick will be O.K. for our Locum. I gave him the dates you wanted in July and he will be free then. I think he'll be up to the work. He seemed a bit nervous of the Zoo so he's coming down for a day later on and I'll take him round and give him a few tips.'

'It would be a good thing if we could book him for next year as well,' I said, 'though I suppose he'll be fixed up in a job by then.' A thought struck me. 'Why not take him on as your assistant? You know you're working so hard that you can't do any more and the Practice goes on expanding all the time.'

Maurice shook his head. 'Can't afford to yet. I'd rather wait until the children have finished their education. We'll be a bit better off then; at least, I hope so. Besides . . .'

He pulled off the road and stopped the engine. We sat looking across the fields and, for a moment, he remained silent.

Then he said thoughtfully, 'It's like this: I have a rush of work for a while and then things go quiet for a bit. For instance, here's the spring, soon all the cattle will be out in the fields, consequently not so much illness. The odd calving, of course, but most of the big things happen in the autumn and winter. You know, T.B. testing, blood testing for brucellosis, de-horning and so on. We are getting more small animals now, of course, with whelping cases and bitches to be spayed and, if we get some hot spells of weather, then the dogs and cats keep us busy with parasites, skin irritations, etc. Horses are always with us and the Zoo is taking up more and more time but, when I get a quiet period, I shouldn't want an assistant hanging around doing nothing and getting paid for it.'

'That's not the point, he would be doing what work there was including night calls and you would be able to take things more easily.'

Maurice looked at me in horror. 'Can you see that happening? It would drive me mad. I like my work. Do you want to turn me into an old codger before my time?'

'Oh! Well, one day you'll have to take somebody in. A partner, perhaps.'

'A partnership is like marriage,' Maurice grinned, 'a very dicey business. You have to go into it thoroughly before you take the plunge.'

I thought back to our lightning courtship. 'You should know, and, talking of marriage, how much will you bet that Bill and Mary become engaged this weekend?'

'I never bet on certainties,' Maurice pulled the self-starter, 'but I can tell you where he'll stage his proposal.'

'I know – down in the piggery!'

It was late that evening that Bill telephoned. 'I thought you'd like to know that Mary and I are engaged.' His voice broke with emotion. 'I asked her when we went down to look at the pigs again. I've loved her from the moment we met but now that I know she likes pigs as much as I do, it makes things absolutely perfect. She doesn't mind in the least that I'm only a farm manager.'

When he had rung off, Maurice got out a bottle.

'We must drink their health,' and then, as he filled the glasses, he paused and chuckled, 'I shouldn't be surprised if they even spend their honeymoon in the piggery!'

Chapter 9

I handed the receiver to Maurice as he came into the room. 'It's from Parklands Stud. The manager says one of their most valuable mares has just foaled but there's something wrong with the colt.'

Maurice nodded, took over the telephone and I stayed to listen. 'The foal can't stand? Same trouble as last time? I'll be right over.'

He turned to me. 'Coming?'

'Wouldn't miss it for the world,' and I hurried away to get ready.

It was always interesting to go to Parklands. Owned by Sir Miles Stanton, it was situated a short distance outside the county town and, as soon as we shut the big gates behind us, we entered another world. The immaculate gravel drive, flanked by tall trees, led up to the stable block and acres of well-kept paddocks. Here, horses reigned supreme and were the sole topic of conversation.

The foaling took place early in the year and it was always one of our favourite family outings when we went to visit the new arrivals. But this was a late foaling and the stud manager's face was mournful as he led us towards the stable.

'We saw it directly he was born. He'll never be any good. He'll have to be shot.'

Maurice said nothing but stood looking down at the little colt. While we watched, he began trying to struggle upright. Once, twice, three times he tried to make it but it was no use. As he fell down on his knees I saw that his front feet were deformed and he was quite unable to straighten them.

His mother nudged him up again, her soft brown eyes puzzled and anxious, but the foal whickered sadly and collapsed once more in a little heap.

Maurice knelt in the straw and passed his hands gently down the foal's legs. 'Back tendons too short,' he said, 'he can't possibly straighten his fetlocks. Same as Stardust had five years ago.'

Mr Maitland nodded gloomily. 'Yes, and we know how that ended.' He turned away, 'I'll go and ring the knacker now.'

'No. Wait . . .' Maurice stood up quickly, 'since that last one I've done a bit of research and I think I've got the answer.'

'What do you mean?' Mr Maitland asked impatiently. 'You know we've no money to spare for experiments.'

'This won't cost anything.'

I saw the expression in Maurice's eyes and knew he would do anything to save that little foal. 'If it doesn't work I won't charge a penny.'

He turned the foal gently towards him. 'He's a lovely little fellow, I'd like to have a shot at saving him.'

The foal looked at him timidly as if seeking reassurance. Once more he tried to stand and his mother, watching his struggles, moved uneasily. 'All right, old lady, don't fret. We'll see what we can do.' Maurice patted her nose and turned to Mr Maitland, 'Now this is what I have in mind.'

I moved away to stroke the foal but I heard the manager say incredulously, 'Shoes? Where would you get them that size?'

'I've got them already,' Maurice pulled out a notebook and began to draw. 'I had them made some while ago. They're in a cupboard in my Surgery waiting for just such an occasion.'

He pointed to the diagram. 'This ring is welded on to the toe of the shoe. Then there's a strip of very thin metal, about an inch wide, with a hook welded on to the end of that. The shoe is nailed on to the foot, which must be forced out straight by hand, then the hook is put through the ring . . .'

Mr Maitland interrupted, 'I get the idea but I don't think it will work. You'll never get the shoes nailed on. The hoof will be too thin and soft.'

Maurice frowned, 'That, I admit, is my chief worry. But the only way to find out is to try.'

Mr Maitland stroked his chin and stared down at the foal. 'I don't know what Sir Miles will say. You know what a perfectionist he is. If a foal's not right at birth he has no further use for it. It's a pity he's in America now but perhaps if I sent him a cable asking . . .'

Maurice shook his head impatiently. 'Listen,' he said, and I knew he was determined not to be beaten, 'if this foal is to be saved, the treatment must start at once, before the tendons have hardened. If we leave it twenty-four hours it will be too late.'

Behind him the foal was pushing the straw about as he continued his pitiful struggle and my heart contracted at the thought of what lay ahead for him and his mother.

At last Mr Maitland said thoughtfully, 'Sir Miles particularly wanted this foal because of his breeding. I'd like to save him if possible but . . .'

'No "buts"!' Maurice ordered and slapped him on the shoulder, 'I'll get those shoes and come back as soon as you've got the farrier organised.' He strode off towards the car and I realised that he had completely forgotten I was there.

Mr Maitland looked at me. 'Your husband's crazy, but I suppose I'd better let him have his head.'

When I caught up with him, he was sitting in the car drumming his fingers on the steering wheel.

'When are you going back?' I asked.

'I'll give him about an hour. He should have got the farrier by then. I hope he's available, there's no time to waste. Are you coming along to see it work?'

'I don't know,' I said doubtfully, 'I couldn't bear it if . . .'

'No "ifs" either,' Maurice said calmly, 'it's got to work. That little foal is not going to the knackers if I can help it.'

As soon as we reached home, I went into the house to check up on everything and then made a quick cup of coffee. A few minutes later Maurice joined me, carrying a small box. He held it out to me and I took off the lid.

The little shoes were the smallest I had ever seen. No more than two and a half inches across, each with five tiny holes for the nails. I admired them but said nothing. How could that poor little creature possibly keep them on?

Maurice read my thoughts. 'It's going to be difficult but Jim is a good farrier. He'll do his best.' He looked at his watch. 'Let's get going.'

When we arrived at the stables, the farrier, a burly red-headed man, was already there, standing talking to Mr Maitland outside the loose box. Maurice got out of the car. 'I know,' he smiled, 'you don't think it can be done.'

'Well,' the man hesitated, 'I reckon the hoof'll split and I don't know that I've got any nails small enough for what you want.'

Maurice handed him the shoes and the farrier shook his head. 'Nothing small enough,' he repeated.

Suddenly, Maurice grew irritable. 'Well, file some down then,' he said abruptly and turned away to stroke the mare's nose.

Mr Maitland said, 'It's all right, Jim. He gets like that if he's frustrated.'

The farrier smiled understandingly as he opened his canvas bag and searched for his file.

'By the way,' Mr Maitland took out his wallet, 'I sent off a cable to Sir Miles just now. This is what I said: "Colt foal to Moon Rider. Similar deformity as Stardust. Beginning treatment." That should give you a few hours' grace.'

Maurice looked at him gratefully. 'Thanks, you know this means a lot to me. I'm sure it can be done.'

We stood waiting until the farrier had finished the nails and then we went into the loose box. They worked quickly. The little foal struggled at first, then lay passive on his side with the firm, gentle hands holding him down on the straw.

The mare moved about restlessly and Mr Maitland spoke soothingly, 'It's all right, old lady, we won't hurt him.'

Fifteen minutes later, the farrier looked up. 'Well, they're on – but only just. Only two nails in each shoe are actually holding. It may be enough.'

Then Maurice took over. Slipping the hook through the ring in the toe of the shoe, he instructed the farrier: 'Get the foot out as straight as you can while I bandage this strap on to the foreleg.'

Ten minutes later they stood back.

'Now, my lad,' said Maurice and I heard the tremor in his voice, 'let's see what you can do on those.'

At first the foal lay still, then, gradually, he began again his hitherto hopeless battle. But this time it was different. I held my breath as I watched him put his front legs straight out, then, with a bound, he was standing on all four feet for the first time in his life.

Not daring to move, we stood there in silence as, slowly and unsteadily, he went over to his mother and began to feed.

I felt a great lump in my throat and stealing a glance at Maurice, I saw that his eyes were moist.

He turned to Mr Maitland. 'Make him walk as much as possible. His weight will stretch those back tendons better than anything. I'll look in tomorrow.'

Driving home, Maurice said nothing for some while then he muttered, half to himself, 'I'd like him to go out into the paddock tomorrow for a couple of hours. I know it's a bit soon but, thank goodness, it's turned warm at the moment.'

Giving up all pretence at housework, I went with Maurice the next day and watched when the foal was let out into the paddock with his mother. He stood in amazement when he saw the vast expanse of green, then, gradually, a little stiffly and clumsily, he began to frisk about.

'So far, so good,' said Maurice, 'but we shan't really

75

know anything till we take off the splints.'

Mr Maitland then warned us, 'I had a cable this morning. Sir Miles says treatment is useless. I'm to put the foal down.'

'We may yet have to,' said Maurice grimly, 'but we'll keep our fingers crossed.'

For the next three days the foal continued to grow stronger. He took little gallops up the paddock on his own as he became bolder and bolder. Although slightly impeded by his splints, he began to run around with the other foals and apart from the fact that he couldn't bend his fetlocks, there was little to choose between them.

On the morning of the fifth day, Mr Maitland telephoned. 'The nails are out of each shoe.'

'I'll come at once,' Maurice replied, 'we'll have to take them off now.'

When we arrived the foal was resting on the ground. Bending down, Maurice undid the bandages, then, carefully, he removed the splints and pulled off the little shoes.

Once more he stood back. 'Now you're on your own, old chap.'

Without any difficulty the foal got up and stood gracefully beside his mother.

There was silence for a minute or two, then Maurice said, 'That's fine. His own weight will do the rest. In a couple of days he'll be as sound as a bell.'

Mr Maitland beamed, 'Sir Miles will be delighted. You'll be able to name your fee.'

Maurice smiled, his eyes on the little foal prancing gaily at his mother's side, 'I've got my reward already.'

Chapter 10

It was going to be a hectic weekend. Our friends the Masons were coming over from Canada and, before going up north to visit their families, they had promised to spend a couple of days with us.

When I say 'friends', I mean Peter Mason alone. We had known him for many years, ever since he and Maurice had worked together as assistants in a large Practice immediately after qualifying. After a while, he grew restless and decided to set up on his own. He worked very hard for a year or two then sold up and went off on a tour of exploration. He wanted to find the best country in which to settle and, a bachelor with no ties, it was easy for him to wander round the world. Eventually he decided on Canada and was now married to a Canadian girl we had never met.

Immediately I heard they were coming over, I looked at the house with critical eyes and it seemed to me that the whole place needed redecorating from top to bottom.

Pointing this out to Maurice, I received little sympathy. 'It's only your inferiority complex working overtime as usual, you always go on like this when we have visitors.'

I thought about this for a while and came to the conclusion that there was something in what he said. My uneasiness arose from the fact that I am not very house-proud, absolutely no use at 'Do it Yourself', have no knowledge of the latest trends in furnishing and am a very ordinary cook.

This last is my greatest worry. When things are going along in everyday routine with no emergencies or threatened calamities, I get by with what is known as 'plain cooking'. But, when I am nervous, my cooking, such as it is, goes all to pieces.

Sometimes, under the impression that this is the right thing to do, visitors come into the kitchen and ask to help. Others just stand watching. This is even worse and behind my fixed smile my teeth are clenched and my light, airy manner hides a blood pressure roaring up towards a cerebral explosion.

Now it seemed I was going to have an efficient housewife watching me do the idiotic things I always do when efficient housewives watch me. I knew she would be terribly capable because of the way in which Peter Mason, in the days before he went to Canada, used to test the wifely potential of every girl he met.

I remember one occasion when he was having tea with us and I found, much to my indignation and Maurice's amusement, that I had just been subjected to one of his examinations. This was based on the theory that, as soon as the tea cups were filled, the teapot must be refilled immediately with boiling water. If the unfortunate girl failed to do this within seconds, he took it as a sign that she would be thoughtless and imprudent with no care for the future.

Peter explained all this to us at great length, then passed his cup to me for a refill. It was then that I found, much to my chagrin, that the tea pot was nearly empty. Although I did not come under the heading of candidate for the Mason name, I found it hard to bear his reproachful looks and the pitying glance he gave Maurice.

Presumably his wife had survived all the little traps he had set for her and was the paragon he sought. I made a mental note to keep her out of my kitchen at all costs.

'Peter has done very well in Canada,' said Maurice, the evening before their arrival. 'In his last letter to me he suggested we might join him over there. How would you like that?'

At first sight, it seemed an attractive proposition and I was all prepared to start packing, but I knew it wasn't as simple as that. The personalities of Peter and Maurice, both attractive in their different ways, would not mingle well enough for a partnership.

'I know,' Maurice said, reading my thoughts, 'but it will be interesting to hear about conditions in Canada.'

The next day started badly.

John and Margaret overslept, were late down to breakfast and left in a mad rush to catch their bus; the telephone rang with maddening frequency and, although Maurice had promised to try and manage his morning Surgery without me so that I could get on with my preparations, there were so many people in the Waiting Room that this plan had to be abandoned.

As if that weren't enough, when the last client had departed, we were left with a cat to be spayed and a dog needing to be operated on for a bad obstruction due to eating bones.

Maurice decided to do the cat first so, whilst he was scrubbing up, I went to lift the big tom out of the basket where he had been a very indignant prisoner.

'Careful!' Maurice warned, as the cat laid back his ears and showed his claws, but he spoke too late. I looked ruefully at the long gash down the back of my hand but I knew better than to let go of the animal.

'I'll give you something to put on that,' I was promised but we had to do the anaesthetising first.

The operation was soon done and the cat popped back into his basket.

There was another cat basket standing against the wall and Maurice said, 'Remind me to take that fellow with me when I leave. He's O.K. now and I promised to take him back to his home this morning as his owners can't get in to fetch him. I'll go there first and then work my way round the farms. Now, if you'll just help me get this dog anaesthetised, I'll manage alone and you can get on with your own work.'

Immersed in my chores, I was thankful that the telephone did not ring for two hours and, when it did, I picked up the receiver with the feeling that at last I had got everything under control.

'Mrs Dawson here. Isn't Mr Bowring coming this morning? We've been waiting in all this time and he said he'd bring our cat back first thing after Surgery.'

I stared down at the telephone. What on earth had happened? He wouldn't drive around with a cat any longer than he could help. I assured Mrs Dawson that he must have been delayed and I expected he'd be with them soon.

Then I got down to the serious business of worrying. I looked at the list of farms Maurice had to visit and rang the first one.

No. He hadn't arrived yet. They hoped he wouldn't be too long as they'd kept the cows in specially.

The next half-hour was utter misery with my imagination working overtime. Then the telephone rang again.

'Oh! Maurice!' I was overjoyed, 'What's happened? Are you all right?'

'I'm perfectly O.K. but I've done the damnedest, silliest thing. I've lost the cat! The window was open a few inches and he forced his way out of the basket and was through the window like greased lightning. He shot across the road into a wood and I've been searching and calling for ages. I've just been to tell the Dawsons.'

'Oh! My goodness!' I was so horrified I nearly dropped the receiver, 'How did they take it?'

'They're furious, of course. They've gone off to the wood themselves to see if they can find him. Now I'm off on my rounds. I shan't be home to lunch.'

When he finally arrived home I went out to welcome him and saw, as he got out of the car, that he was limping badly.

'It's all right,' he said, 'I'm still alive though I was beginning to think I wouldn't get through the day. A mare kicked me when I was making a rectal examination for pregnancy. She caught me just above the knee. Luckily she hadn't got any shoes on. I've got some stuff I'll rub in to get out some of the bruising.'

He went upstairs and a few minutes later came into the kitchen where I had some sandwiches and coffee waiting.

'What a day! I shall have to go and see if I can help the Dawsons find that damn cat. What time are the Masons arriving?'

'Not till seven thirty, but we shan't be eating until about eight fifteen.'

'Right!' Maurice emptied his cup and got up stiffly, 'I'll be off. Mind you, the Dawsons are so angry they'll probably tell me to go to hell.'

His car drove in about an hour later and when I heard the jubilant toot on the horn, I knew the cat had been found.

'Damn funny!' Maurice laughed, 'I went straight to the wood and the Dawsons were still there, armed with saucers of food and looking quite desperate. Finally, I persuaded them to let me drive them home and, although they could hardly bring themselves to speak to me, they agreed. It was only half a mile or so away but it was a very uncomfortable journey because Mr Dawson kept saying what a fool I was to have had the window open and, of course, I couldn't deny it. Mrs Dawson sobbed quietly into her handkerchief and I wished I were dead. Then, as we pulled up outside their house we saw Timmy, curled up on the door step waiting patiently to be let in. My God! What a relief!'

He looked at his watch. 'Ten minutes before evening Surgery – let's have a drink.'

'To celebrate finding the cat,' I said.

Maurice grinned wryly, 'And losing a client. The Dawsons won't come to me again.'

By the time our visitors arrived we were feeling quite light-hearted and we settled down to enjoy our guests.

Sylvia Mason was charming. Smart, friendly and pretty and, although I knew she must be terribly efficient she kept that side completely hidden.

After dinner we discussed Canada and British Columbia in particular. It was, they told us, the most wonderful country for a Veterinary Surgeon.

Peter – now Dr Mason – was already a power in his little community. When, five years ago, he put up his plate in the small town about a hundred miles from

Vancouver, he found that the animals poured into his Surgery.

'I hadn't even got a table to examine them on when they started arriving,' he said. 'Now I have two cars and a yacht and I employ an assistant who is looking after the Practice while we are away.'

When the conversation turned at last to our own plans Maurice mentioned his difficulties in getting Locums.

Peter looked disapproving. 'It's all so unnecessary. Why tie yourselves down here? Sell your Practice and come out to Canada. You need only to pass a small exam which would enable you to work in Canada. You'd never regret it. There are plenty of little towns like ours just crying out for Vets if you don't want to come in with me.'

As the talk went on I listened and wondered. Was this going to be another of my 'Let's go and live there' phases?

I had had so many of these periods of unrest and each one took its toll. Admittedly, while the flame is burning, it is all very exciting and I learn a tremendous amount about the country of my current choice. But, when it is all over, how flat, how dull everything seems for a while. Until another part of the world presents itself in alluring colours and I am off, figuratively speaking, once more.

Coming probably from my Scottish forebears, there lurks in the depth of my being the germ of Wanderlust. Locked up, starved of real nourishment, treated scornfully and rarely permitted to see the light of day, it is surely the most frustrated little germ that ever existed and it is a wonder that it manages to survive at all. It is, however, very, very tough. Periodically it tunnels up and listens to our conversation.

At the first whisper of another continent, a word of praise for another way of life – little Wanderlust is there and then there is no holding him back. After weeks and sometimes months of rising temperatures and fever-pitch excitement during which he really thinks he is about to be indulged at last, the far horizon, so enticingly attractive, suddenly vanishes. Another mirage has come and gone and poor Wanderlust sinks despairingly down again into the depths.

I have been, in theory, to so many parts of the world. Australia – land of sunshine and opportunity, New Zealand – a near thing this, only dropped because of dislike of Veterinary conditions of work, South Africa – short lived, America, even the Caribbean, and in all these places I had imagined living in idyllic conditions. I had faced up to and conquered homesickness by the simple method of becoming so rich that we would be able to afford a long holiday back in England almost every other year.

But there was always the awakening. There were many obstacles between us and the far-off land. Family ties, financial and emotional needs – all these held us back; but underneath it all was the realisation that we loved our own country too much to want to leave it for good.

I really thought that I had settled down at last but, here I was, at it again. Then, suddenly, perhaps some chance word did it, I lost interest in the conversation.

'I'll get some more coffee,' I said, and went out to the kitchen where I stood for a while gazing out into the garden, wondering why I wasn't worked up. What had happened to Wanderlust? Why wasn't I thrilled at the idea of a chance to have a wonderful new life in the great open spaces?

Great open spaces? Well, not exactly. From what I could make out, the life of a Canadian family in a small town isn't all that exciting. It sounded, apart from climate and local differences, very much the same sort of life as in any small town. Hardly worth selling up and starting afresh.

Just then, the kitchen door opened and I turned guiltily towards the stove.

Sylvia came in, 'May I help?'

Then she smiled, and added, 'When people say that to me I go all stupid inside. But I don't suppose you ever feel like that. You're so calm and well organised.'

I gazed at her in astonishment. Well organised? Was that how I appeared to a stranger?

'I expect your Canadian ways are much more efficient than mine,' I said.

My guest sat down at the table. 'Peter is always telling me I ought to take a "Course in Household Management" and I suppose I'll have to, one day, because I'm not exactly the practical type.'

'Tell me,' I enquired with interest, 'what was Peter like when you first met him? Did he put you through any, well, er – tests? Things like watching to see if you put fresh water in the teapot immediately after filling the cups?'

Sylvia gave her attractive little chuckle. 'The teapot test? Yes, he tried that on me once. But he wouldn't tell me what it meant when I forgot the water so I told him if he tried out any more dotty ideas like that I wouldn't marry him.'

Forgetting the coffee, Sylvia and I settled down for a long talk.

Later, when we were preparing for bed, Maurice said, 'You don't seem all that interested in Canada. I should have thought that by now you would have chosen the house, got the children settled in schools and become a real Canadian housewife.'

'That's the trouble, that's why I don't want to go.'

'You – don't – want – to go?' Maurice fell back on the bed in mock collapse. 'You – the intrepid adventuress, the pioneer of the wide open spaces . . .'

'There aren't any,' I said, 'at least, not in the towns.'

'Aren't any what?'

'Wide open spaces. Not round where we would live, anyway. Among ordinary surburban people. They cut their lawns every week at the same time; no fences, so if you don't mow the grass you spoil the whole effect. And they all belong to things: Good Citizens' Club, Amateur Theatricals, Folk Music – why, Sylvia is even studying Christmas decorating at night school. Imagine!'

'No Canada then?' Maurice said slowly, and I wondered if, this time, the roles were reversed and he was the one who wanted to go.

'I expect I've exaggerated a bit. But, although it must be different in the big cities and there are plenty of wide open spaces for holidays, it's certainly pretty narrow in the small towns judging from what Sylvia has told me.'

'It would almost be worth going, just to see you rushing around being a Good Citizen. I must admit though,' he added, with an enormous grin, 'it's a relief to know you feel like that. I can't say I was anxious to hit the trail. There may be gold in them thar hills but I'll settle for the small change here.'

I nodded and smiled, and it was then that little Wander-lust finally curled up and died.

It was, as they say, a Happy Release.

Chapter 11

———◆———

Thursday is Maurice's half-day. What that means is that he gets home late for lunch, having squeezed all his calls into the morning, and, with no evening Surgery, the rest of the day is his, except for anything really urgent.

This particular Thursday we were sitting out on the terrace enjoying the warm spring sunshine and trying to avoid looking at the weeds in the flower beds when the telephone rang.

Maurice automatically began to heave himself out of his chair but I pushed him back and went to take the call. A minute later I put my head through the open window. 'You'll have to come. It's the Zoo and it's urgent.'

Picking up the receiver, he listened attentively and when he said 'I'll be right over,' I knew our peaceful interlude was ended.

He turned to me, 'Simon, the problem chimpanzee, has been hurt in a fight.' And, as he picked up his case, he added, 'How about coming along and forgetting those weeds?'

Simon was a twelve-year-old chimpanzee who spent all his time tormenting and knocking his wife about. It had been almost impossible to get him to settle down in domestic bliss like the other chimps. He had nearly killed his first two wives and they had had to be taken away but, eventually, he had formed a stormy kind of partnership with the third. He used to chase her around unmercifully but, on the whole, she took it in good part.

Occasionally he went too far and then she'd turn on him, chattering and swearing until he flounced off, glowering, into a corner.

Then she became ill and the keepers were about to put her into another cage because of Simon's rough ways when they discovered that he had suddenly changed. It seemed as though he couldn't do enough for her. He tried to tempt her failing appetite by picking out all the choicest tit-bits, the ripest bananas, the best grapes and, if he thought she was thirsty, he took the bowl and held it while she took a few sips. Then he'd nod with satisfaction and stroke her cheek approvingly. In spite of all that was done for her she died in the end.

They tried him out with another mate but he wouldn't have anything to do with her. His old bad temper returned and he attacked her so they had to be separated. Maurice told me how dangerous he had now become – as soon as anyone comes near he bangs on the floor of his cage with his fists, all the hair on his neck and shoulders bristles up with rage and he looks quite terrifying. It goes without saying that I was worried about how Maurice was going to deal with him

The Superintendent greeted us as soon as we arrived and as we walked towards the ape house, he said, 'We've had a real old shindy here. It happened when the keeper – a new man – was cleaning out the cages. He accidentally left the partition up between Simon and his next-door neighbours. It was only a matter of about an inch but that was enough. The moment Simon came back he spotted it. He flung it up in a flash and there he was, face to face with young Donald and Daisy. Simon plunged in and attacked Donald ferociously.'

George explained to me, 'They fight in the most extraordinary way, you know. They take it in turns to grasp the other's arm and chew away at the hand. The one who's being attacked makes dreadful grimaces but doesn't attempt to resist. He just keeps up a continuous barking until it's his turn to chew and bite.'

'Did the female join in?' I asked.

George laughed, 'Oh! No! She crouched in the corner hugging herself, and enjoying every moment. When her mate was pulling and gnawing at Simon's hands, she egged him on, calling out, "Ugh! Ugh!" and then when it was Simon's turn, she rocked backwards and forwards with excitement. She didn't care who won.'

Maurice was concerned. 'Simon isn't as young as he was. Didn't you try to stop the fight?'

'Of course we did,' George said indignantly, 'we shouted and lunged at them with long poles but it wasn't as easy as that because of the cage bars, and it took some time. Then Simon began to realise that his first youth was over and, although he's enormously strong, he soon found he was fighting for his life. The young chimp was defending his mate and that gave him extra strength. He began biting Simon's shoulders and the back of his head and it was awful to hear him screaming in triumph. Eventually we managed to separate them long enough to let Simon creep back into his own cage.'

Simon was lying down but, as soon as we approached, he got slowly to his feet and lumbered up to the front of the cage looking quite pitiful.

Maurice talked to him softly, 'What have they done to you then, poor old boy?' And Simon, all his savagery gone, responded to the sympathy in Maurice's voice. He fixed his mournful eyes on him and held out his hands like a child.

I watched in amazement as Maurice took them gently, turned them over and looked at the deep gashes and bruised flesh and, all the time, he kept up his soothing talk to which Simon replied with sad little noises and, as if trying to tell what had happened, gave little jerks of his head towards the next-door cage.

Maurice took out a tube of ointment from his case and carefully smoothed it on to the wounded hands. Then he felt round the back of Simon's head and the chimp turned obediently to allow him to spread it down over his shoulders. A bunch of grapes was produced and Maurice inserted an antibiotic tablet into one, which Simon took and swallowed. He was then given the rest of the bunch and, as he solemnly picked them off the stalk, he looked at Maurice and George almost lovingly. Then, treatment over, he went into his sleeping quarters and settled down again.

'He's a reformed character,' I said.

But George shook his head. 'I wouldn't bank on that.'

The young chimp next door had injuries to his hands only but, filled with the headiness of victory, he was unco-operative so his drinking water was laced with antibiotic, much to his disgust.

Maurice turned to George. 'I'll come in tomorrow and have another look at Simon. It will be interesting to see how long he will continue to be so amenable.'

It lasted for about ten days. During that time Simon revelled in the sympathy he received from all around him. As soon as anyone approached his cage he went to the bars and showed his hands, turning them over and over for inspection. Then, as his wounds healed, his aggressive nature reasserted itself.

He began snarling at his keepers who, recognising the signs, took care to avoid any more physical contact with him. Soon he was as difficult and dangerous as before but, even then, something seemed to linger in his memory. For a long time afterwards, whenever Maurice appeared and said, 'Hello, Simon. How are those poor old hands?' the angry eyes would soften for a few moments. A minute later, however, snarling and baring his teeth at his former friend, he was completely unapproachable.

Simon ill and Simon well, were two different creatures.

Chapter 12

Maurice held open the car door. 'You won't mind, will you, if I pick up a dog on the way?'

I glanced involuntarily at my navy blue suit, and he added, 'It's a black Labrador and, in any case, he can go in the back.'

'So long as he doesn't decide to be sick all over my collar, like that Alsatian a few weeks ago. Goodness! What I have to put up with one way and another! Here we are, just going out for a quiet drive . . .'

Maurice grinned unsympathetically, 'What a life you lead! But, seriously, this Labrador is a beautiful animal. About six months old, strong, healthy and gentle. His owners want him put to sleep.'

I was shocked. 'Why, for heaven's sake?'

'They're tired of him. He was lovely as a pup but now he's getting a nuisance, needs exercise – they live in a small flat – and also he needs a dog licence. That,' he added grimly, 'is usually the most important reason.'

We drove along in silence for a while, then Maurice said, 'It's almost impossible to find a home for a dog at such short notice, but I think in this case . . .'

He broke off as we drew near a large block of flats. 'This is the address,' he said, and switching off the engine, he sat for a moment in thought.

'Some time ago the cowman over at Meadow Farm asked me if I could get him a dog. He left the choice to me;

only stipulated that the animal should be good with children.'

'Why, that's just the thing. What a bit of luck!'

'Don't be too sure, these people may insist on the dog being put to sleep. Ethically, I'm bound to do as they ask.'

'They wouldn't insist, surely,' I said indignantly, but Maurice gave a wry smile.

'Well, there are some very odd folk around. Also, the cowman may have changed his mind. I haven't been to the farm for some time. He may even have found a dog elsewhere by now.' He opened the door. 'Anyhow, I'll see what I can do.'

Ten minutes later he came back to the car with a leggy young Labrador pulling reluctantly on the lead.

I opened the door beside me. 'Let him sit here. What's his name?'

'Jet.' Maurice waited for the dog to jump in but he was nervous and hung back. Finally he lifted him up and I put my arm around him. I spoke soothingly, trying to make him relax and, at last, he gave a little sigh and seemed to settle down.

As we drove off, Maurice said, 'It's all right so far. His owners don't mind what I do with him. Keep your fingers crossed.'

Soon we reached the lane leading to Meadow Farm and pulled up outside a cottage. Maurice walked over to Tom who was working in his garden. I could hardly bear to look in case I should see Tom shake his head but I needn't have worried. In no time at all Jet was out of the car and surrounded by the whole Jarrett family, father, mother and three children.

'Never thought you'd get me such a fine little fellow,'

said the delighted Tom. 'He'll make a grand gun dog too.'

Mrs Jarrett smiled at me, 'I've got the kettle on. Will you come in and have a cup with us?'

We stayed there about an hour and by the end of that time Jet had already become a member of the household. The children took him into the meadow behind their cottage where he raced around in ecstatic joy and Tom was already making plans to take him out rabbiting.

We were nearly home when Maurice said, 'After being confined to bricks and mortar, Jet has been transported into a dog's Paradise. I feel as pleased about it as I do when I have performed a successful major operation.'

'I can understand that,' I said, 'and I suppose in a way, you have.'

'Have what?' Maurice sounded puzzled.

'Performed a major operation. And what's more, it has certainly saved Jet's life.'

'I wouldn't say that. I couldn't have put him to sleep once the owners had said they didn't mind either way.'

'I know, I was thinking along those lines when I was waiting in the car. We would have kept him ourselves. All the same, we don't really want another dog just yet.'

'No. But it's always difficult when a case like this comes along, so thank goodness the Jarretts wanted him. I haven't forgotten what it was like in our early days.'

I laughed as I remembered that we simply weren't able to say no. There was the little mongrel stray someone brought into the Surgery and he had such a mournful look that we couldn't resist him. Then the puppy abandoned in the woods and Hamish, the tom-cat who ruled everybody and that terrier with the broken leg – the place was getting overrun.

Maurice continued, 'But there comes a time when you have to decide whether you are a Veterinary Surgeon or a home for unwanted animals.'

'Judging from what I've heard from other Vets' wives, it seems to be an occupational hazard. Mrs Walker told me the other day that the last straw for her was a raven. A relation brought it back from Cornwall with a broken wing. As soon as it was O.K. they gave it its freedom but it has become so domesticated that it keeps flying back into the house and tearing the place to pieces.'

'This "humanising" of wild creatures is sometimes a great mistake,' said Maurice. 'There's a case now at the Zoo. A little monkey has been kept as a pet ever since it was a baby and brought up in the home like a child. Now the owners can't cope with it so they asked the Zoo to take it in. George told me he was very reluctant but he accepted it and it has been a tremendous problem. It didn't know it was a monkey.'

I laughed, but Maurice insisted, 'No. I'm quite serious. It was terrified of its own kind. They put it in with the others and it went stiff with fear and screamed terribly all the time. It had to be taken out of the enclosure every ten minutes. Then it would rush into the keeper's arms, trembling and crying so much that they thought the poor little thing would have to be put to sleep. Eventually it lost its fear and seems quite happy now though I expect it's a very mixed-up monkey inside.'

It was after Surgery that evening that I realised we had the old problem once more. The last client had left and Maurice looked down at a cat basket on the floor. 'I've got a feeling that I've been "conned". Do you remember that man who came in this morning, asking us to spay this kitten?'

I nodded, 'A new client – well – I'd never seen him before, anyway.'

'That's right. He didn't leave his name or address. Just said he'd pick the kitten up this evening. We were a bit rushed at the time. Well, he hasn't turned up to collect it.'

'He may have been delayed,' I said.

Maurice frowned, 'I don't think we'll see him again.'

'But why not? If he didn't want the kitten why bother to have it spayed?'

'Well – think!' Maurice said impatiently. 'When clients have an animal put to sleep they pay straight away, don't they? When it's spayed, they pay when they collect it.'

'What a rotten trick!' I was furious. 'Putting the kitten through an operation and taking up your time . . .' I broke off and watched as Maurice opened the basket and took out a little white kitten of about three months old. It was fully conscious and immediately tried to scratch Maurice's hand but he took it firmly in his arms and stroked it gently. 'It's terribly thin, half-starved. Let's find it some food.'

It went for the milk and some chopped-up bits of chicken as though it hadn't had a meal for a week and I was all for giving it more but Maurice stopped me. 'Don't overdo it, do you want diarrhoea all over the place?'

I looked at him suspiciously, 'So we're going to keep it?'

'Well, we've got to look after it for a day or two anyway. The man might turn up eventually. What else can we do?'

He put the kitten down and it backed away into a corner glaring at us like a miniature tiger. 'It's very wild,'

I said, 'almost as though it had been badly treated.'

'I expect it has. Probably given to children as a toy and been tormented until it scratched in self-defence. Then it is condemned out of hand as a bad-tempered animal and thrown out. It may have kept coming back to the only home it has known so they've stopped feeding it. And now they've thought of a smart way out of their difficulty.'

'And we're landed with it.'

'I tell you what we'll do,' Maurice suggested, 'we'll keep it for a while, feed it up and see if it gets less wild with kind treatment, then we'll try and find it a good home.'

The kitten settled down fairly well, gradually gaining confidence. At first it responded to affection with sharp little bites and scratches but it mingled its attacks with purrs and slowly became more gentle. When our dog appeared, though, the kitten immediately reverted to her former imitation of a wild cat. Robert was mildly interested in the newcomer but, at the sight of the arched back with bristling fur, the pink mouth with tiny, sharp teeth bared at him and the hiss of warning, he withdrew to a safe distance where he lay, full length, his nose on his paws, studying the little white ball of fire glaring at him.

We had had the kitten about a fortnight when Maurice came back from answering the telephone. 'The Convent cat is on the way out. It's very old and can't possibly recover. I'll just nip over there now.'

I didn't go with him because, much as I liked the nuns, a visit to the Convent was a time-consuming event. The Sisters ran a home for old ladies and looked after them so well that the old ladies seemed to live for ever. Spending their lives among the aged and infirm, the nuns were always delighted to see young people and John and Margaret were great favourites. There was always a welcome for us no matter when we called and time seemed to stand still from the moment we rang the bell.

First of all, there was the ushering in by the nun who opened the door. After making a fuss of the children, commenting on their rate of growth and demanding news of their progress at school, she showed us into the parlour where we waited patiently for the arrival of Reverend Mother. When she entered, followed by a retinue of Sisters, we all sat down again to answer questions concerning our welfare and our latest doings. Then, delving into her capacious pockets, Reverend Mother would find, much to her pretended surprise, little parcels of sweets, which, when the children were small, were received with great delight. Even now, although Margaret and John were teenagers, the same jelly babies and chocolate buttons would be produced causing a certain amount of adolescent embarrassment but generally eaten on the way home.

Then came the tour of the house where we duly admired the budgies in the old ladies' sitting room and more nuns appeared to chat with us.

After that came a visit to the kitchen where the Sister Cook produced home-made cakes and then we were taken outside to see the goats, chickens and the dog who was the particular pet of Sister Clare who looked after the gardens.

We admired their work immensely and Maurice never charged them any fees but, not to be outdone, they showered us with gifts at Christmas including an enormous, beautifully iced cake which lasted us for weeks.

When, however, Maurice called in his professional capacity, the nuns appreciating that his time was limited never held him up unnecessarily, so on this occasion it wasn't long before he returned.

'I've had to put the cat down, and there's great lamentation among the old ladies. There's a good home there for White Kitten but I didn't say anything in case you want to keep it.'

I pondered for a while. We had all grown fond of the little creature but it would have a good life with the nuns and be thoroughly spoilt.

'I think they'd better have it,' I said, at last, 'I've no doubt it won't be the last refugee we shall take in.'

'That's true,' Maurice grinned. 'As a matter of fact, there's a baby gibbon at the Zoo. Its mother has died and they're bringing it up on the bottle. Would you like to take that on?'

'Very funny! The day you bring a monkey into this household will be the day I walk out. You have been warned.'

Maurice chuckled. 'I can take a hint. But, as a matter of interest, where would you go?'

'That's easy, I'll go and live in the Convent with the old ladies and White Kitten.'

Chapter 13

It looked like being a quiet Sunday. Breakfast had been leisurely with no telephone calls and we sat drinking our coffee and reading the papers in unaccustomed peace.

'A perfect April morning,' Maurice said, 'and marvellous weather for the bees.'

'Let's hope we get a good crop of honey this year,' I said. 'What are they working on at the moment?'

'They'll be gathering pollen for the new brood, I hope. Let's go and see.'

He led the way across the lawn to the end of the garden where he keeps four hives. Going up to the first one, he stood watching the comings and goings of the inmates but I kept at a safe distance. I know my place where bees are concerned and it is as far away from them as possible. Luckily, our garden is large and the hives are tucked away in a warm, sheltered corner facing away from the lawn where we sit.

'Look,' Maurice called, and I ventured a bit nearer, 'see those yellow lumps they're bringing in on their back legs – that's pollen. It means the queen has survived the winter and is laying. The pollen which is rich in protein is for feeding the larvae. They'll soon be working on the apple blossom and the sycamore trees and, with this weather, we should get a good honey flow later on.'

He pointed to the farthest hive. 'That one is empty. The queen died in the winter. I'd like to get hold of an early swarm and start up a new colony.'

Suddenly I turned away. A bee was buzzing angrily round my head and I knew from experience that it would soon be followed by several more. Bees just don't like me and the feeling is reciprocated. But I have to admit that it is well worth while keeping them because we have a constant supply of honey and, although we eat a tremendous amount ourselves, we still have plenty left to give to friends and relations.

The weather continued warm and in the middle of May we had a really hot spell. The 'honey flow' was on and the bees worked madly. Whenever Maurice had half-an-hour to spare he would place a chair near the hives and study their activities, sometimes giving me a running commentary.

'Unbending with the bees' he called it and, although I would have preferred him to mow the lawn or do a bit of weeding, I hadn't the heart to tear him away. It was, he said, the perfect relaxation, watching about a hundred thousand workers slaving away for him.

He was sitting watching them one Thursday afternoon when I answered the telephone and then went out to give him the message. 'It's the Convent, they've got a swarm of bees in their garden. It's settled on the branch of a tree and the old ladies from the Home are getting fearfully excited and are swotting the stray ones under the impression that they are wasps.'

Maurice shuddered. The swotting of bees came, in his opinion, under the heading of crimes worthy of capital punishment. 'Tell them I'll just collect my equipment and I'll be right along. Would you like to come with me?'

I hesitated, 'Are you going to bring them back with you?'

He shook his head. 'No. All I have to do is to put the swarm into a skep and let the bees settle down. I'll pick them up in the evening. What a bit of luck it's happened on my half-day.'

'Why do they say "A swarm of bees in May is worth a load of hay"?' I asked as we went out to the car.

'Well, it's obvious. It means the new colony has a chance to build up and gather honey before the end of the season. That's why the value diminishes as the months go on, "a swarm in June – worth a silver spoon" and "a swarm in July – not worth a fly".'

When we arrived at the Convent the old ladies had retreated indoors and all was peace in the garden. Sister Clare greeted us warmly and led us to a small tree where the swarm hung, a dense vibrating mass of golden insects.

'It's quite a good one,' said Maurice, 'just what I needed for that empty hive.'

He was putting on his veil, hat and gloves when Sister Clare said, 'Would you mind waiting a few minutes? Reverend Mother is coming and she would like to see you take the bees.'

I smiled to myself. Reverend Mother never missed a chance of seeing something new and Maurice was going to have an admiring audience. A few moments later a group of nuns came across the grass, laughing gaily at the prospect of this exciting event.

Maurice grinned. 'I expect you're all hoping like mad to see me get stung.'

Cries of horrified expostulation greeted this and Reverend Mother chuckled, 'Well, it would certainly add to the excitement,' and the nuns laughed approvingly.

Maurice pointed to his veil. 'I've put this on because I

don't believe in taking chances, but, as a matter of fact, bees very rarely sting at the beginning of a swarm. They are filled with honey and are in a good mood. It's a kind of holiday for them. About the only one they'll ever have.'

He placed a round straw skep immediately underneath the hanging mass and gave the branch a firm, sharp blow. A few bees flew out wildly but the bulk of the swarm fell like a great sponge into the basket. Quickly Maurice turned it upside down. Then, picking up a piece of brick, he propped up one side of the skep.

'Now, if the queen is there, as I think she is, they will form up into another mass, hanging from the roof. If, by any chance, she isn't with them, they will all come out in search of her.'

He stood watching closely. 'Yes, she's there all right. Come and see this.'

He pointed to a little group of bees, about half-a-dozen, who had come out on to the edge of the skep and were standing on their front legs with their rear ends right up in the air.

'They're opening up the scent glands in their tails and fanning furiously with their wings to guide all the stragglers to this new location,' he explained.

Then, looking at his watch, he said, 'I'll be back at sunset just to gather them up and take them to the new hive. They won't zoom off then as they will be anxious to stay under cover. A swarm won't fly after dusk.'

After tea, we went back to the Convent. I took a bit of persuading to go along with Maurice but he assured me that no bees would escape into the car, so although I had my doubts, I took the risk.

When we arrived the audience had increased. Evidently

Reverend Mother approved of this kind of instructional entertainment for the Community.

This time Maurice had brought with him a small, white sheet and he put this on the ground near the swarm.

Gently lifting the skep, he put it face down on to the sheet, brought up the sides and tied them round the rim to stop the bees getting out. Then he carried them over to his car and put them carefully on the back seat.

'How do you get them into their new home?' asked Reverend Mother as the nuns gathered round to say goodbye.

'Well, there are various methods but this is the way I do it: outside the empty hive I place a board at an angle to the ground, making a run-up to the entrance. Then I drape this sheet over the board and on to the ground, lift up the skep and tip the swarm on to the sheet. A few bees will run up the slope and go into the hive to inspect it. When they come out, they return to the main body of bees and then there will be a slow, concerted movement to the entrance. The next thing is to watch for the queen. It's easy to pick her out on the white sheet.'

'How on earth can you recognise her?' asked Sister Clare.

'You can't miss her, she's much bigger than the others – a good inch in length – and she has reddish coloured legs. Once she is in, it's only a matter of about half-an-hour or so before all the bees are in their new home.'

As we got into our car, Maurice asked Reverend Mother, 'Why don't you keep a few hives here? You've got plenty of room. I'll come along, if you like, and tell you how to begin.'

Reverend Mother nodded her head thoughtfully. 'The

honey would certainly be very good for our old ladies.'

Maurice smiled as he started up the engine. 'Fine,' he said, 'and, if you can stop them from swotting the bees, I shall feel I haven't lived in vain.'

Chapter 14

———◆———

Maurice came into the house looking vaguely irritated. He poured himself a drink and sat down sighing as though he had had a tiring morning.

'What's up?' I asked. 'Something gone wrong?'

He shrugged his shoulders. 'I've just been to Beechcroft Farm.'

I knew what that meant. 'Joyce again, I suppose.'

He nodded. 'She really is a terrible battle-axe. Tom Watson can't call his cows his own. She won't even let the poor man into the cowshed at milking time. Says he upsets the animals. And when I had to give an injection today she started to query my treatment.'

'But I thought she was such a marvellous herdswoman,' I said. 'Last time I saw Tom Watson he was singing her praises like mad.'

'Oh! yes, she's good, and two years ago when she took on the job, Tom knew he'd found a treasure. But, if you remember, that was during his wife's last illness and Joyce was left to manage everything. She adores those Jerseys and won't allow any interference with her way of looking after them. That's all right up to a point but Tom Watson has been a farmer all his life and he knows as much, if not more, about cows as Joyce. Like all experts they often disagree – violently. Then he says he's going to sack her but never does and Joyce says she'll leave but never goes.'

I laughed and thought back to the first time I saw

Joyce. I guessed her age at about thirty and remembered that she made me think of a Viking. Tall, sun tanned, with very blue eyes and beautiful corn-coloured hair. She was always immaculate in fresh white overalls and the confident way she handled the herd of Jerseys filled me with admiration. The cows were lovely creatures with sleek, shiny coats and pretty little faces and they were the pride of Tom Watson's life. It must be very galling for him, I reflected, to have them taken over so completely by his own herdswoman.

'Why is he so weak with Joyce?' I asked, 'you'd think he'd be able to stand up to her. He doesn't strike me as a coward.'

'He's not. But they have these fearful rows and she always seems to win.' Maurice grinned, 'Of course, his wife was a terrible nagger and I suppose he's used to giving in. He's been a lot happier since she died. Joyce is the fly in his ointment now. Well, not exactly a fly – more like a hornet, I should say.'

'What was the trouble today?' I asked, 'is there something wrong with the herd?'

'No. It was just a routine injection but Tom asked me to settle an argument. It was to do with the amount of concentrates Joyce is giving to the cows whilst they are being milked. He said she thinks nothing is too good for them but he wasn't in farming for his health and would I try to convince her that she's far too extravagant.'

'That's his job,' I said indignantly, 'he's the one who employs her, not you.'

'I know. Anyhow, I went and looked at the milk yield charts on the wall and asked her exactly how much concentrate she was giving them. She glowered a bit but she had to tell me eventually and, of course, it was far too much. I told her that if she went on increasing it like that it would affect the cows' livers and then she went away in a huff. Tom said, "She'll give in her notice when you've gone and a damn good job too." It made me feel a bit awkward. I don't like being called in to settle their grievances.'

Later that day when Maurice was out on his calls, Mr Watson rang. 'Just wanted to thank your husband for settling that argument for me this morning . . .' then he paused, 'Joyce has given in her notice.'

'Well, perhaps it's for the best,' I said cheerfully, 'you'll soon find someone else to take her place.'

'Almost impossible,' he said gloomily, 'she's one in a million. Don't know what I'll do without her.'

I tried to ignore his pessimism. 'Will you get a relief milker while you're looking for the right person?'

'I can't do that. Joyce would never come back if I did. She always finds fault with them when I've had them during her holidays. She says the cows haven't been stripped out properly or the milking machine hasn't been thoroughly washed. There's always something wrong.'

'But I thought you wanted her to leave?'

'Well . . .' Mr Watson sighed, 'you know how it is. I don't want her to go really – just like her to get a bit more reasonable.'

I gave up and, promising to pass on his message, I put down the receiver.

They must have settled their differences because Joyce stayed on and, a few weeks later, Maurice was called in to see a cow that Joyce said was due to calve at any moment.

The weather had changed. We seemed to be back in the

winter with icy winds and driving rain and when Maurice returned he looked frozen.

'That stupid woman!' he exclaimed, shaking out his coat and sending a shower all over the kitchen, 'she's going to sit up all night with that cow. I told her there wasn't the slightest need because it won't calve tonight. I examined it per rectum and the cervix is completely closed. She knows I'm right but she's just pig-headed. As a matter of fact, I thought she was looking pretty seedy. She's overworking and, with all this 'flu about she's asking for trouble.'

'Oh! Well, let her get on with it,' I said heartlessly, 'I've lost patience with both of them. Let's hope you don't get called out again today in this foul weather.'

But he was unlucky. About 2 a.m. the telephone rang and he had to go to a whelping case. Unable to get back to sleep I went downstairs to put on the kettle and wait for his return. But it was nearly dawn when, at last, tired and soaking wet, he arrived home.

'High drama at Beechcroft Farm,' he said.

I looked at him in astonishment. 'What on earth . . .? I thought you went out on a whelping case.'

'I did. It was all over pretty quickly and on the way back I passed Beechcroft Farm. I felt a bit uneasy about Joyce and wondered if she really was sitting up with that cow so I drove quietly into the yard but, of course, the dogs began barking. I turned round quickly and was going to drive off when I saw a light in the cowshed. It was too early for first milking so I investigated.

'Sure enough, there was Joyce but, to my horror, she was lying on the floor! Unconscious!'

He paused, made sure that I was suitably enthralled,

then went on, 'I got Tom Watson out and we picked her up and drove her down to her cottage. Then we waited for Dr Jackson. He said it was a collapse caused, no doubt, by overwork and self-neglect, and she also had a touch of pleurisy.'

'Well, well,' I said, 'I'm very sorry for her and all that and I hope she'll soon be O.K. but right now I want you to go to bed. You're the one who's overworked.'

The next thing we heard was that Tom Watson had sent his daily help down to look after Joyce and that Tom himself was doing the milking and visiting Joyce every day to report on the cows.

'He's on top of the world,' reported Maurice, after seeing him one day. 'Must be the effect of his new-found authority. And Joyce, apparently, is a changed woman.'

'In what way?' I asked, wondering whether a battle-axe could be changed into anything else.

'Apparently she's overwhelmed with gratitude to Tom and she's also told him her life story. She looked after an invalid brother for years until he died and Tom says it's not surprising that she turned a bit sour after an experience like that.'

'I scent romance in the air.'

Maurice stared at me incredulously. 'Honestly! You women! I know you love to matchmake but that's ridiculous.'

'Why?' I asked calmly, 'she's a good-looking woman and he's a middle-aged widower – very suitable.'

Maurice shook his head despairingly. 'You're crazy.'

But a few weeks later he returned from a visit to Beech-croft Farm looking stunned. 'You were right, Tom Watson and Joyce are going to get married. When he told me I could hardly believe my ears. He must be mad. First wife a nagger and the second one a battle-axe.'

'I thought you said she was a changed woman.'

'Well, that was when she was ill but she's gradually getting back to her old self and I can see trouble ahead. Tom says he's not going to allow her to overdo things again and he's going to engage a cowman for the herd. It's got to be a man this time, he says, and I can see his point.'

Filled with curiosity, I rang Mr Watson the next day to congratulate him on his engagement. 'I hope you'll both be very happy,' I said. And then added, 'Does Joyce mind giving up the herd?'

'I soon settled that,' Tom Watson's voice was proud and confident. 'We had a little bit of an argument but I told her she could always do relief milking and I think she's realised that they will be her cows as well as mine once we're married.'

'That's marvellous,' I said, 'and a happy solution to all your problems.'

Tom Watson chuckled, 'You're right there.'

I put down the receiver and gave Maurice the gist of the conversation. 'Not my idea of a great romance,' he remarked, 'and there's one thing that puzzles me.'

'What's that?'

'I can't make up my mind whether Joyce is marrying Tom in order to get the cows or whether he's marrying her in order to get rid of his awkward herdswoman.'

'We shall never know, but I wouldn't like to be the new cowman.'

Chapter 15

We were on our way to the Zoo when Maurice told me he was glad I was coming because he wanted me to see Lola, the tigress, who had become extraordinarily friendly. She and her mate Sam lived in a state of armed neutrality because although Lola was pretty easy going, Sam was savage and unstable.

Some weeks before he had attacked her and had taken a chunk out of her back. The wound was about eight inches square. Maurice had decided to treat her while she was conscious so that she could feel that he was helping her. As the wound had to be dressed each day until it healed he couldn't have given her an anaesthetic every time. It would probably have damaged her liver and her general health. At first she was so badly shaken up that she hardly realised what was going on, but on the second day, when she had recovered from the shock, Maurice was rather apprehensive about how she would react. Fortunately she was quite willing to let him attend to her. He dressed the wound and began to pet her, rubbing her behind the ears and stroking her under the chin. And, after several days of treatment, she came up of her own accord and placed herself against the bars as soon as he arrived.

'Now,' Maurice said, 'she purrs away whenever I go to her and we're almost on nose rubbing terms.'

'Are you going through that performance again today?' I asked, feeling rather alarmed but trying not to show my apprehension, because I know that building up a good relationship with a wild animal is an achievement dear to Maurice's heart.

'It's healed up now but she's as friendly as ever. To tell the truth, I drop in there most days now, simply to keep up the bond between us.'

'I suppose she's grateful.'

But Maurice shook his head. 'I don't think animals ever really feel grateful. In my opinion, that is purely a human virtue. The real link that binds us together is trust and it must be mutual. You see, in the wild state, animals always know who is on their side but they have an instinctive distrust of man. It's only when you have extra contact with them that this fear can be overcome. Up to a point, mind you, because if you go too far, suspicion will return. An animal in a cage is cornered and a jerky or uncontrolled movement – anything sudden – and the link is immediately broken. It's chiefly fear that causes the change.'

'But surely all wild animals aren't alike. You told me the other day that the young male leopard is getting very uncertain and yet he was so friendly and lovable as a cub.'

'That's true. Leopards, in fact, seem to be the exception to the general rule that wild animals will avoid contact with man. In their case, fear is almost non-existent and their main characteristic is their ferocity.'

As we turned into the Zoo gates Maurice added, 'I believe Lola is going to be turned out into the paddock today so it will be interesting to see if she will remain friendly with me. We'll go and see her first. Then I've got to take out an elephant's tooth.'

'What?' I stared at him in consternation, 'how on earth are you going to do that?'

'Well, to tell you the truth, I don't quite know myself. Last time I tried to look at it she got a bit fed up and showed a tendency to get me up against the wall and lean on me. But George and I will work out something between us. Don't worry.'

Stunned into unusual silence, I walked with him towards the tigers' enclosure wondering ruefully whether it wouldn't have been better to have stayed at home. Watching my husband rubbing noses with a tigress and endeavouring to pull out an elephant's tooth was a little more than I had bargained for.

As the Superintendent came towards us, the sight of his calm, relaxed figure gave me confidence. I stopped envying my friends with husbands who went regularly to their offices and spent their weekends playing golf or gardening and decided that being a Vet's wife had something after all. It was different at any rate, and tigers and elephants were great topics for conversation when things got dull at a party.

'Lola's very pleased at getting out into the open again,' said George, 'and Sam is delighted to see her. Perhaps they'll live in peace for a while now.'

Maurice climbed over the barrier and stood against the wire mesh enclosing the paddock.

Lola was at the far end but, as soon as he called her, she came bounding towards him and flung herself full length against the barrier. Slowly and carefully Maurice stroked her under the chin and I could hear quite plainly her vibrant, swelling purrs of pleasure. It was lovely to see the friendship between them and I almost envied Maurice the thrill of caressing that beautiful coat. I saw him gently feeling the place where she had been bitten and

then, suddenly, she turned on to her back and he r
her tummy while she rolled from side to side.

At last he came away, saying, 'The wound's
Healed beautifully. I'm almost glad it happened.'

Seeing the pleasure on his face, I knew just how h

'I hope,' remarked George cheerfully, as we went
the elephants' enclosure, 'that Betty will be a
operative as Lola was. But she's not at her best a
moment. It's a tooth that should have dropped
naturally but it's got twisted sideways in the mouth

Maurice explained, 'It won't require much streng
extract it because the roots aren't very deep.
sequently, we don't need any anaesthetic. The probl
how to distract her whilst I wrench it out. It's right a
back of the mouth, too.'

'Lumps of sugar.' George produced a tin. 'Look
put them one at a time on her tongue and you n
those steps, you may be able to whip it out quickly.

I held my breath as Maurice climbed up to the le
Betty's mouth but she showed no interest in the force
was holding and kept her eyes on the sugar lump G
was holding out enticingly. It looked highly perilo
me – she had only to swing her massive head roun
Maurice would be thrown to the ground – but with
concentration he gazed searchingly into the cave
mouth whilst George calmly counted as he dole
Betty's favourite sweets.

'Four,' he said, 'now, hold up your head, Betty
reach for this one.'

And, suddenly, I saw Maurice give a quick, stron
and, as he withdrew the forceps, I saw the great lu
ivory.

To my surprise, Betty showed no resentment and seemed to understand that something that had been hurting her was gone. With renewed zest she returned to the sugar lumps and Maurice descended from his perch and held out the tooth.

It was about seven inches long and about three inches deep, completely smooth on the biting surface and with only a little blood on the roots that had been still holding. A rather unpleasant object I thought, but Maurice was delighted.

He weighed it in his hand. 'About two and a half pounds, I should think. When I've cleaned it up it will make a very nice addition to my collection.'

When Betty had received her last lump of sugar, George shut the tin and moved away. Then, seeing her working her trunk round and round, he turned hastily to warn Maurice. But he was too late. With a little snort – almost, it would seem, a giggle – she ejected a squirt of mucus all over him catching him completely unawares as he stood admiring her tooth.

'Blast!' Maurice looked at his jacket in disgust. 'Oh! well, I suppose I got off lightly all things considered.'

'That tooth looks very old,' I said, 'will she get another or is that her second set?'

'They don't have their teeth like that. Apart from their tusks they have only four at any one time, one on each side of the upper and lower jaw. These wear down, get quite smooth like this one here and normally fall out, to be replaced by new ones. They have, on average, a total of about fifteen.'

'She was really very good this time, wasn't she?' said George. 'But then she knew something was wrong and that you were going to put it right.'

'That's true,' Maurice nodded, 'but do you remember when, a few weeks ago, I needed to get a blood sample from her for a laboratory test. She wouldn't co-operate then. Because she wasn't in any discomfort she didn't consider there was any need to allow me to take liberties with her.'

'Where on earth can you take blood from an elephant?' I asked. 'Is there any special place or do you just shove in the needle and hope for the best?'

'You certainly do not. The only place is from a vein just behind the ear but, when I attempted it on that occasion, she knocked me around with her trunk and flattened her ears tightly against her head. It took me well over an hour to get what I wanted and then it was only by a fluke. A camel was being led past her compound and her curiosity caused her to drop her guard long enough for me to get the needle into the vein.'

'Yes, well, she didn't see the point of it,' said George, and laughed heartily at his own joke. 'But,' he went on, 'if you remember, when she had that little growth on her trunk she was very patient. Let you put on the local anaesthetic and your operation went off without a hitch.'

'There's no doubt about it, elephants certainly have powers of reasoning and they're subject to moods too, like us. When Betty feels irritable it's no use trying to jolly her up. She has to be left alone until she recovers her good temper.'

We continued our tour of the Zoo with Maurice and George discussing various problems and deciding how to treat them – a course of vitamins for this animal, a future operation for that one – until, at last, footsore and weary, I felt I had seen all I wanted of the animal world. But Maurice, engrossed in his work, would have gone on for ever if time hadn't prevented him and seemed surprised when I heaved a sigh of relief as we finally got into the car.

'Had enough?' he asked and I nodded ruefully.

'Sometimes I think it would be nice never to see another animal again, and it would do *you* good to get away from them sometimes. How about going up to town with me on your next half-day? Do some shopping.' I looked distastefully at his jacket, 'You need some new clothes, anyway.'

'Oh! This will clean up all right,' said Maurice cheerfully. 'You go – you need a break – but you know how I hate all those crowds milling around. Give me a herd of cows any time!'

'You really do like animals better than people?'

'Yes.' Then he added hastily, 'With the exception of my family, of course.'

Chapter 16

Periodically I do what is known as 'clearing the message pads'. We have three telephones, two in the house and one in the Surgery and each has, or should have, a message pad with ball point pen or pencil beside it. Highly organised and efficient. At least, that's the general idea, but, in a household like ours, the only place where efficiency reigns is in the Surgery.

Naturally, we are all extremely telephone conscious and to leave the bell ringing for any length of time is considered a major crime. Consequently, the receiver is apt to be lifted upstairs as well as downstairs with resulting confusion to the caller who very often gets two or even three people saying 'Hello' in succession. Occasionally – and here I am often the offender – having taken a call upstairs, you have to run downstairs for information and the first receiver is forgotten and not replaced. This leaves you with such a feeling of guilt that you go around for days afterwards looking closely at every telephone just to 'make sure'.

Pens and pencils, even when attached to the telephone by every conceivable gadget, tend to disappear, loose sheets of paper get tucked under the telephone and nothing stays tidy for long.

All these little things mean that the system is in frequent need of an overhaul and I usually combine the job of putting everything in order with the task of going through all the old messages and transferring vital information to the main telephone list in the Surgery. This is tedious work and each time I reproach myself for not doing it sooner, thus avoiding doodles over the previous day's messages and dealing with half-torn sheets with part of someone's name on them and nothing else, which always gets me worried.

In our family we have decidedly individual styles when it comes to transcribing information from the telephone.

Maurice is economical and to the point. The surname and address of the caller, the animal concerned and only an occasional doodle when the client on the other end is long-winded. Unfortunately, like most medical men, his handwriting is practically illegible and although, by now, I ought to be able to decipher it, it still defeats me and I end up trying to copy the scrawly bits at the end of each word hoping he will be able to solve the puzzle.

Any message that John takes is usually complicated by his peculiar method of spelling. Although it might meet with the approval of progressive teachers who consider good spelling to be old fashioned and unnecessary, hand-outs such as 'daksund with diaorea,' or 'heffer with newmonia,' are liable to provoke furious demands from his father as to why he is pouring out enormous fees for his son's so-called education.

Margaret's communications are erratic because, unwilling to bother with details, she merely puts down a telephone number and adds 'please ring'. When this results in bitter enquiries from Maurice as to who is paying the telephone bills, she takes her revenge next time with masses of irrelevant information and the query 'is this enough?'

I flatter myself that my messages cannot be faulted.

Unfortunately, I tend to branch off into shorthand when the client is very talkative thus bringing down on my head sarcastic requests for a translation.

However, in spite of everything, the work gets done somehow and I was hard at it the other day when the telephone rang and I listened to a particularly feather-brained client. Out of sheer interest to see how the conversation would look on paper, I took it down in shorthand and then, consumed with mirth, I transcribed it into longhand for Maurice's benefit.

I had just finished when he came in and I handed him the sheet of paper. 'Do me a favour,' I said, 'read it aloud.'

Puzzled but obliging he did as I asked:

CALL TO SEE DOG.

'Yes, this is Mr Bowring's house but I'm afraid he's out on his calls.'

'Oh. Well, perhaps you could give me some advice.'

'I can take a message. I'm only the Vet's wife. I'm not qualified to give advice.'

'Still, you must see a lot of what goes on. I expect you know nearly as much as your husband.'

'I'm afraid that isn't so. If you like to give me your name and address I'll get my husband to call if you wish.'

'Tell him it's Mrs Walton and that Jackie is being sick all the time.'

'Mrs Walton of where?'

'Mrs Walton of Knightsford. You see, Jackie hasn't been well for several days and . . .'

'Could I just have the rest of your address, please?'

'What? Oh, yes. Meadow Road. As I was saying Jackie . . .'

'Meadow Road is a long road. Could I have the number of your house?'

'It hasn't got one. It's called "Chez Nous" – French, you know.'

'I see. Will you be in all day, Mrs Walton?'

'Oh, yes. I wouldn't leave Jackie. I'm devoted to him – he has the best of everything.'

'Is Jackie a dog or a cat?'

'Why, a dog, of course! My cat's called Fluffy.'

'Oh!'

'I'm sure I don't know why Jackie keeps on being sick. I'm most particular about his food. He never has anything I wouldn't eat myself.'

'Dogs shouldn't have fancy food.'

'Oh, I know. I only give him plain food, plain cakes – never cream doughnuts, just the ordinary jam ones – plain bread and the best butter. He won't look at margarine. Turns away in disgust. I always say, breeding tells. And he's rather naughty about chocolate – must have his little bar after every meal and won't let me forget it.'

'Oh, dear!'

'And then, of course, he has meat. Twice a day I cook for him – a steak at mid-day and for supper something tasty like a pork chop or a little fried chicken.'

'You must tell my husband all about Jackie's diet and then I expect he will soon discover the reason for his bouts of sickness.'

'Well, *I* can't understand it, anyhow. And, although I'm sure Mr Bowring does his best, I don't feel very satisfied.'

'I'll give my husband your message, Mrs Walton.'

'Thank you. By the way, tell him that Fluffy – the cat, you know – is a bit off colour too, and that Joey, the budgie, seems rather droopy. So he can see them at the same time and then it won't cost me any extra.

'Goodbye. Wait a moment, tell him – Mrs Bowring, are you there? Oh, bother! She's gone.'

Maurice put the paper down and stared at me. 'You led her on,' he said accusingly.

Disappointed at such a poor reaction, I said, 'Good Lord! Don't you think it's funny? Where's your sense of humour?'

He still didn't laugh. 'Oh! It's funny all right. Of course it is. But I have to look at it from the animal's point of view. The poor little brute doesn't stand a chance. I've tried and tried to get through to that fool of a woman that she is being cruel to her dog but it's no use. People like that aren't fit to keep animals.'

He picked up the message again. 'I tell you what, if you will type it out, put in a fictitious name and address and change the animals' names also, I'll frame it and hang it up in the Waiting Room with a comment from me underneath and hope that clients like Mrs Walton may get the point.'

The telephone rang and he went to answer it.

A minute later he called out, 'For heaven's sake! Where's the pad?' and as I rushed to the rescue, I realised that once more I had fallen down on the job.

I said as much when he replaced the receiver but he only grinned. 'That's the worst of a wife with her head in the clouds. How about coming down to earth and giving me some lunch? Something on the lines Mrs Walton gives her Jackie. You know – a steak or a pork chop or even a little fried chicken?'

'You'll be lucky, it's a ploughman's lunch for you. Bread and cheese and beer.'

'I think,' said Maurice, 'I'll ask Mrs Walton if I can change places with Jackie. She shows her devotion to her loved ones by giving them the best of everything.'

Chapter 17

———◆———

Horses, as Maurice had said, 'go on' all the time and, in his Practice, they range from racehorses to the circus ponies at the Zoo. When they are being bought or sold they have to be given a certificate of fitness. For years I have made appointments for him to do this 'vetting', but it was only when friends of ours told us they were going to buy a horse, that I decided it would be interesting to watch the procedure.

'And procedure it is,' said Maurice, as we drove to the stable where the horse was kept, 'it's all laid down by the Royal College of Veterinary Surgeons and the British Veterinary Association and it mustn't be varied. It will take about an hour. After that, the Gordons want us to go back to their place for tea.'

Michael and Susan Gordon were a middle-aged couple with no children. A few years ago they left London when Michael's health broke down under the stress of life as a senior business executive, settled down in a small house with a few fields attached and surrounded themselves with animals. Susan had taken up riding and the mare she wanted to buy was at a neighbouring stable where she and Michael were waiting when we drove into the yard.

After introducing us to the owner, Susan turned to me and pointed out the chestnut mare standing in the loose box.

'Isn't she lovely? Just what I want. Do you know, I've

never seen a horse vetted though I expect you know all about it.'

I shook my head. 'It's the first time for me too, so Maurice can give us a running commentary.'

Maurice agreed amiably, 'The things I get let in for. Never mind, I'll treat you like a bunch of students but I don't want any questions while I'm occupied.'

We took the hint and stayed silent as he went into the loose box armed with an instrument with a light at the end.

'This is an Opthalmoscope. I'm going to look at the internal part of the mare's eyes.'

A few minutes later, he put aside the instrument, opened the mare's mouth and looked at her teeth.

'She's about six years old,' he said to the owner who nodded agreement.

'Now I'm looking round the sides of the mouth for any sores or ulcers, feeling under the chin for old abscesses and under the jaw bone.'

Then he began passing his hand down the mare's legs, beginning on the left hand side of the front, pressing the tendons and bones and doing the same on the back of the leg.

Then he picked up the foot. 'I'm examining the "frog", it's a sort of "rubber" pad that acts as a cushion to absorb shock. Now I'm going to articulate the joints to see that there is no pain or roughness. It's all done in a certain way. If you notice, it's like this: one front leg, one back leg and while coming round from the front I examine the back itself for sores or tenderness. Then I look at the other side of the back when I come round the other way.'

At last he seemed satisfied and turned to the owner 'I want you to walk her up a hard bit of road, as far a that tree over there, then turn and bring her back at trot.'

We withdrew to a distance and watched the girl bring out the mare and Maurice, his eyes never leaving the animal, explained, 'I'm looking at its action and possible signs of lameness.'

He held out his stethoscope as the mare returned with the girl running alongside, and listened to the animal's heart.

'Right, now saddle up and ride her at a canter round that field for about a quarter of an hour. Then bring her straight up to me and pull to a halt. I must listen to the heart and lungs while she is blowing hard.'

As we stood watching the horse and rider, Susan admitted, 'I had no idea it was such a thorough examination. I had a vague notion that you looked at the teeth and walked it up and down and that was that.'

'That's the worst of you city-slickers,' said Maurice with a smile, 'you think that everything to do with animals and the country in general is easy and simple.'

'Not so much of the "city-slickers",' Michael cut in, 'we're learning fast. Do you know, I've sawed up enough logs to last us for nearly two years. The longer I live in the country the more I find that romantic things like log fires and looking after animals mean damn hard work. But it's the kind of work that's made me fit again.'

'More work than ever if you take on a horse,' said Maurice. 'Who's going to do the "mucking out"?'

'I am,' said Susan, 'and don't try to put me off. I want that mare badly. Have you nearly finished the vetting?'

'Not yet,' said Maurice, looking at his watch, 'I must take its markings next and then a final walk and trot to see if any stiffness has developed after this last exercise.'

He called out to the owner to bring up the mare.

As soon as she drew up opposite him, he applied his stethoscope, listened carefully and seemed satisfied.

He then produced a long sheet of paper and showed it to us.

'You see,' he said, 'it's like two maps of a horse – one for each side and the front and back of the legs. Now you see that white blaze on the mare's head? That goes in here in red. Those saddle markings over the withers and right ribs – those I put in red, too. There are no markings on the limbs. There's one inside the coronet – that's the bit of leg just above the hoof – and on the left foot. Nothing on the right or left hind hoof. Those are all natural markings. Now for the acquired ones like scars, etc. Well, there aren't any. There are no physical abnormalities either, likely to impair the animal's usefulness as a hack, which is what Susan wants her for. There that's done. Now,' he turned to the waiting girl, 'will you just walk her up and trot her back again, please.'

He watched carefully until she returned and then, satisfied, said, 'O.K., the vetting is over.'

The Gordons were delighted and, after arranging to pick up the mare next day, they led the way back to their house.

'What would happen,' I asked as we drove along behind their car, 'if, between today and the time the Gordons take over the mare, something bad occurred – she fell and hurt herself or got cut on barbed wire or something?'

'Well, then my vetting would be out of date. The certificate I shall give them tomorrow will be only up to and including the actual time at which my examination took place. You must know that – after all, *you* type out the certificates.'

'I ought to know, but I must admit I don't always work out the whys and wherefores. I expect my mind is on higher things.'

'Such as . . .?'

'Well, fixing up our holiday for instance.'

Maurice groaned. 'Oh! Lord! I thought it was all settled. Dick is coming as Locum and we're going to a cottage by the sea. When you find it, of course.'

'That's just the point,' I said gloomily, 'I've written off about several places but the children aren't very keen. They want to go farther afield. What's more, they say they don't want to spend all day on the beach and won't have anything to do if the weather is bad.'

Maurice sighed with relief. 'Thank goodness for that. It's not my idea of fun, either. Let's try and think of something else.'

We turned into the drive of the Gordons' house and pulled up outside the door.

'Come along in,' said Susan, 'you mustn't take any notice of the general untidiness. We had some people in last night and I haven't got around to clearing up yet. These friends of ours spent the night here on their way back from Scotland where they've been on a fishing holiday. Apparently, they had a marvellous time which pleased us because we recommended the hotel to them.'

Scotland. A fishing holiday. The answer to our problem! I tried to catch Maurice's eye and saw that his interest was already aroused.

Years ago, when he had been working as an assistant, with alternate weekends free, he had been able to indulge in his favourite sport – trout fishing. He used to say it was one of the best forms of relaxation but, when he acquired his own Practice and was perpetually on call, his rods were put aside.

That evening we put the idea to Margaret and John and were delighted to find it greeted with enthusiasm. Soon, Maurice was tying up lines, looking out his favourite flies and lures and giving lessons in casting out on the lawn to the children. We were all set. In a month's time we would be up in the Highlands.

Chapter 18

———————◆———————

I was working against the clock. Three days before our holiday and here I was, ironing like mad and in none too good a temper. To think that only a fortnight ago I had had a beautiful pile of clean clothes all pressed and ready for packing, carefully hidden away. I had remained deaf to cries of: 'Where have all my shirts gone?' – 'Why can't I wear my new jeans?' – 'I can't find my favourite Tee shirt' – and hung grimly on to my precious hoard.

But all to no avail. Emergencies had arisen, my hiding place had been raided and my plans for a calm beginning to our holiday had gone up into outer space.

Into the bargain, the word had gone round that we were going away and, as usual, all the clients who knew had instantly decided that they must have their pets examined, injected, their diets discussed and even their toe-nails cut before we left.

In vain did Maurice assure them that his Locum was perfectly capable, probably brilliant, better perhaps than he was himself – they still poured into the Surgery demanding refills of 'that mixture of yours in case Flossie gets ill when you're away' – 'do you think they have enough pills to last them out' – and 'could you do that spay or hysterectomy now instead of when you come back'.

I was beginning to wonder if a holiday was worth all the fuss, when Maurice came in and sat down at the kitchen table.

'What a day!' he said. 'Thank goodness it's nearly over.'

I wrinkled up my nose in disgust. 'You've brought some of your work home with you. I always know when you've been dealing with pigs. How about changing that jacket?'

He looked surprised. 'What's wrong with a pig smell? A good, healthy aroma with a bit of a tang, I always think. Rather like some of those "outdoor men's" after shave lotions.' He took off the jacket, 'Anyway, if you could drop it into the cleaners tomorrow it will be ready for when I get back.'

I sighed self-pityingly then took a quick look at his trousers. 'Those had better go as well, cow dung.'

'Pity!' He grinned at my irritated expression, 'It's a great mistake – cleaning it off, I mean. It acts as a lure for dogs. Fascinates them and even the most belligerent ones become friendly as they sniff around me. It helps my image. You know, "The dog simply adores him, my dear".'

He got up and filled the kettle. 'What you need is a strong cup of tea. Things have come to a pretty pass when a wife tells her husband he smells.'

Soon I was feeling better tempered but the subject remained in my mind. 'What,' I enquired curiously, 'would you call a really bad smell?'

'Raw onions,' said Maurice promptly.

'No, no,' I shook my head, 'that's just one of your fads.'

'Not at all, I find it utterly revolting. How you can bear to chop them up, I can't imagine.'

'Well, put that aside for the moment. I mean the horrible smells you come up against in your work.'

'Well, now . . .' Maurice pondered for a while, 'a blown cow when I have to puncture it and gas comes hissing from the rumen – some farm hands run for miles – and I'll admit that it makes me turn away for a few seconds. Then, of course, I've often seen cowmen choking over a cleansing that's gone rotten but I can't say that affects me very much. The small mammal house at the Zoo,' he grimaced at the thought, 'now, that's really something. The Keeper calls it "The Perfumery". And the water in the Hippo's pool in winter quarters just before it is due to be changed – that's rather unpleasant. Oh, yes, and mink – I don't like treating them much because, when handled, they pop off their glands and windows have to be opened in order to be able to breathe.'

'How do you get used to it?'

'Well, it's not due to any failure on the part of my olfactory nerve. It's simply a matter of control. Sometimes, when you know you can stand the smell yourself, you can have quite a bit of fun.'

And he started to reminisce about the time he had had to do post mortems on two elephants at the Zoo. They had been moved, with the aid of a crane, up on to the top of a hill where the holes had already been dug for their burial. It had been difficult to open them up because the skin was very, very tough and, by the time he had been able to make a small incision with his sharpest knife, a crowd of spectators had gathered. Maurice could have warned them it was going to be unpleasant, especially as they were downwind, but he didn't. He carried on, cut right down the length of the belly and pulled out some of the bowels. They were so blown up that he had to lance them to let out the gas. It caused an absolute panic.

Maurice laughed at the memory of it, 'They couldn't get away fast enough. I was really rather pleased because, having been poisoned by the public feeding them rubbish, the elephants were able to have a last revenge.'

'Nice,' I said, 'but I'm glad I wasn't there. What were you doing today that made you smell so much?'

'Nothing special. I had to do a post mortem on a sow over at Red Barn Farm. Poor old Bert had to steady the corpse on its back. He took care to keep well upwind but he didn't like it much, whereas I found it only mildly unpleasant. I think I must be pretty well immune by now.'

'Now we're back to pigs again,' I said, 'I still think it's one of the worst smells.'

Maurice shook his head. 'That's because you haven't met the others. I'll admit, of course, that a freshly opened pig manure heap is a bit ripe but it's no worse than some of that French cheese you like.'

I began to laugh. 'What a conversation for the tea table.'

Suddenly Maurice reared his head like a dog on the scent of a pheasant. 'Now, that's awful!' he exclaimed. 'Absolutely foul!'

He got up and went over to the gas stove. 'It's gone out! And if there's one thing I simply can't stand, it's the smell of escaping gas.'

He turned to me reproachfully, 'And you never even noticed it.'

Chapter 19

We were off to Scotland. All packed into the car, the dog between John and Margaret, fishing tackle, luggage and a varied assortment of drinks and fruit to sustain us in between stops for meals.

For the first part of the journey, Maurice kept wondering if he had told Dick this, that or the other, but at last he began to relax.

'Forget you're a Vet,' I said, 'let's try and get away from the animal world.'

'We won't be able to do that,' said John. 'As soon as we get to the hotel and someone finds out, all the old ladies will start wanting advice about their pussy cats and poodles.'

I was afraid he was right. Memories of parties came to my mind. For some reason, although it is not considered etiquette to talk to a doctor you meet socially, about your ailments and operations, there seems to be no rule protecting Vets. Sometimes Maurice, in self-defence, has had to make some dreadful remark which has caused his questioner to look at him in horror and move hastily away, convinced that he is a sadistic type who is only in the profession for the sheer joy of cutting up animals.

'Why not pretend you're something else?' Margaret suggested. 'An ex-convict or a politician, perhaps.'

Her father chuckled. 'I like your association of ideas. After all, other people don't say what they do for a living. Why should I?' He turned to me, 'You didn't write and confirm the booking on Surgery paper, did you?'

I thought hard. 'No. I remember, it was just on an ordinary plain sheet of writing paper.'

'That's fine, then. We won't let anything out to the old ladies.'

'Hope there won't be any,' muttered John. 'I thought this was going to be a fishing holiday.'

'So it is – at least, some of it,' said Maurice. 'You two are only going to spend a week with us, remember. Then your uncle Donald is coming to pick you up so that you can have some time with your cousins.'

We had decided that this would be a good thing for John and Margaret as they might get bored with us after a few days and their uncle and aunt seemed to keep open house for all the young people in the district.

The journey going up the Motorway was uneventful except for our dog and his phobia about bridges. As soon as we approach one, he becomes restless, rocking his body backwards and forwards and then, as we go under the bridge, he ducks, coming up on the other side with an audible sigh of relief.

'Today,' Margaret decided, 'we'll make Robert lie on the floor, then he won't see the road.' We thought this was a good idea and he settled down happily and went to sleep. We forgot he was even there and were engrossed in conversation when, suddenly, up he clambered on to the seat and sat looking apprehensively ahead.

Sure enough, there was the first bridge and, as Robert began rocking, Margaret put her arm around him. 'You ridiculous creature,' she murmured, and tried to calm him down but as usual he ducked and then looked anxiously ahead for the next one.

John said, 'Perhaps he's got a presentiment or something. I expect one day, just as we're going under a bridge, it will collapse on us.'

'Well, apart from flying, I don't know of any way of getting to Scotland without going under a single bridge,' announced Maurice, 'so we'll just have to take our chance.'

Fortunately, no such disaster occurred and we left the Motorway safely and eventually crossed the Border.

This event always has the same effect on me. All my Scottish ancestry comes to the fore and I become so enthusiastic as to be almost unendurable. Luckily, my long-suffering family are used to this change of personality and listen tolerantly to the tales I tell them of the holidays I spent in Scotland when I was young and the way in which my father, a true Scot, used to bring history alive for us. We children were taken into all the little towns, shown round the ruined abbeys and historic houses while he filled our heads with stirring tales of wars against the English and, with anecdotes of writers and poets, he turned the country into a magic land that, for me, has never lost its enchantment.

Unfortunately, my enthusiasm, though causing great amusement to John and Margaret, tends to become wearing, so eventually I subside and revel quietly in the sounds and scents of the Scottish hills.

The hotel was everything we had been promised. An old, turreted mansion on the borders of a famous river with grounds at the back leading straight out on to the moors. Looking at Maurice, gazing blissfully out of the window at the glorious view, I knew that we had chosen the kind of holiday that would give him the rest and relaxation he needed.

At dinner that night we surveyed the other guests and found to our pleasure that they covered several generations. Some families with boys and girls about the same age as our two, a few older couples who, judging from their talk, were going to spend the evening playing bridge, and lots of fishermen – and their equally keen wives – who came in late and made off again hastily, talking about the evening rise with the eternal optimism of all the fishing fraternity.

It wasn't long before we joined in and although I had been afraid that Margaret and John might soon get bored, it became impossible to drag them away from the water. When I suggested a little local sight-seeing, they made it plain that they were merely humouring me and politely, but firmly, intimated that they would far rather go on striving to attain some of their father's skill than do any of the things I had so carefully planned.

Sometimes, for a change, we went to a loch which, the owner of the hotel told us, was 'just over the hill'. It turned out to be a very steep climb on foot, over bog, boulders and tough, tall heather but, when at last we stood looking down over the beautiful stretch of water with woods running down to little beaches, the effort of reaching it seemed more than worth while.

By the end of the first week, we ought to have been exhausted but instead, we were bursting with health and the trout we caught, when served up for dinner, tasted quite heavenly.

When on Sunday Donald arrived to fetch John and Margaret, they were almost reluctant to go, but buoyed up with tales of their cousins' activities and armed with their fishing tackle – just in case – they went off quite happily.

At dinner that evening Maurice said, 'You've been very patient with all this fishing mania but now it's your turn for a break. Let's go and do a spot of revisiting old haunts. How about going over to the place where we got engaged?'

We drove down to the little village in the Borders, where Maurice had been stationed for several months during the war, just before going overseas. He and his fellow officers were billeted in an old castle and as we approached it, memories came flooding back and all the intervening years seemed to fall away.

I had been with the W.A.A.F. – the Women's Auxiliary Air Force – at Morecambe in Lancashire. Having already met Maurice once in Morecambe and twice on leave in London, it had been arranged that I and three of my fellow W.A.A.F. should hitch-hike up to Scotland on a forty-eight hour pass. The Factor on the castle estate and his wife agreed to put us up and we were going to be entertained by Maurice and his friends at the local pub. Unfortunately, at the last moment, my pass was cut down to twenty-four hours so my friends went on ahead, leaving me to hitch-hike on my own the following day. An obliging lorry driver took me as far as Gretna Green and it was then that things became difficult. Walking along a deserted country road on a bitterly cold November evening, trying to flag down the occasional lorry by dint of waving a white handkerchief – the only method in the wartime blackout – proved singularly unrewarding and gradually it dawned on me that I was

tranded. Soon there were no lorries at all and the only
ounds were those of owls hooting in the woods. I set out
o walk the twenty-odd miles hoping that I would find
telephone booth somewhere along the way. After about
n hour I saw the tiny pinprick of light that buses were
llowed and stood in the middle of the road, waving my
andkerchief frantically in a 'they shall not pass' mood.
My luck was in and the bus put me down in the village
utside the pub just as Maurice was organising a search
arty and about to set off in the Staff car.

I must have looked a very unromantic figure, tired and
irty in my crumpled W.A.A.F. uniform but it didn't
eem to matter because, when the party was over, Maurice
nd I strolled down to the nearby river and there, in a
eautiful setting – a hard white frost, icicles hanging from
he trees and a brilliant moon shining down on the water –
ve became engaged.

It seemed incredible, looking back, that in the very
vorst period of a war that appeared endless, we should
ave had the temerity to plan for the future. We knew
ery little about each other, it was only our fourth meeting,
ut we were young and very much in love.

Three months later we were married and spent a
ortnight together in Scotland before Maurice and his
attalion left to fight in North Africa and all the way up
taly.

We relived it all again as we strolled once more by the
iver.

Our time alone passed only too quickly and soon John
nd Margaret returned full of talk about the good time
hey had had. We toured around, did some more fishing

and then, refreshed and rejuvenated, set off for home.

'It's nice to think that Dick won't leave until tomorrow' I said, 'you'll have the whole evening to relax after th long drive.'

But I spoke too soon. Dick greeted us with obviou relief.

'Everything has been fine,' he reported, 'but, righ now, I've got a crisis on my hands. I hate to bother yo immediately but I'm afraid I need help. There's th bitch coming in for a pyometra – she's fearfully toxic an I think it's touch and go – but that's not all. Mr Rampto the new farmer at Southlands, has found one of his cov dead. It broke out of the field and may have picked u something poisonous.'

Maurice looked thoughtful, 'It may well be yew tre poisoning. When old Mr Miller was there, he lost tw cows that way. There are yew trees in those woods ne> to that bottom field. He had a constant battle with peopl taking a short cut and breaking down the fences. B don't forget, in a case like this when the cause of death unknown, you must first of all do an anthrax test. S you'd better nip over there now, take a blood smear an bring it back here to look at under the microscop Remind Mr Rampton that he can't send the body to th knackers until you've got the result. It's obligatory.'

Dick looked at his watch. 'The bitch is coming in a any moment. That's why I've been hanging aroun when I ought to be at the farm. Do you think . . .?' H paused, 'I know you've only just come home, but . . .'

Maurice said, 'It's all right. I'll do the operation,' an smiled at Dick's sigh of relief.

We just had time for a quick cup of tea and then th

patient arrived. An old spaniel and a weeping mistress. We were back with a vengeance.

'I'm afraid her chances aren't good,' said Maurice, looking up from his examination. 'If she comes through the operation – and she's so toxic that the anaesthetic may kill her – she may have a few more years of life but you would be fully justified in having her put to sleep now. I'm afraid it's your decision.'

There was a long silence. I looked at the owner and saw the anguish in her eyes. Turning away, I busied myself tidying up the bottles on the shelves, then I heard her say, 'What would you do if she were yours, Mr Bowring?'

Maurice hesitated. He took another look at his patient and, at last said gently, 'I'd let her go now.'

There was another silence and my heart went out to the poor woman. Finally, she said, 'I suppose I'm being selfish but I'll take the chance. I know you'll do your best.'

He did, but it was no use and eventually he went to the telephone and broke the news.

He turned to me, 'I shan't charge her for the operation.' And then, looking down at the dead animal, he added despondently, 'Not a very good start after the holiday.'

Glancing out of the window, I saw Dick's car coming into the drive and soon Maurice and Dick were examining the blood smear.

'No trace of anthrax bacillus there,' said Dick, 'you're obviously right about the poisoning. The cow was lying right beside a yew tree, anyhow. I believe it's almost instantaneous, isn't it?'

Maurice nodded, 'You'll find some yew leaves when you open the stomach.'

At last, we all sat down to a belated meal and Dick, who had evidently enjoyed being our Locum, talked at length of the work he had done. I listened vaguely, my mind on other things, and finally he said, 'I'm awfully sorry. I haven't asked you yet – did you have a good holiday?'

'Wonderful!' Maurice smiled across at me. 'We regained our lost youth and now we're ready for anything.'

I thought of the washing and ironing that lay ahead. 'Well – nearly anything.'

Chapter 20

We had only been away for a few weeks but it seemed to me that we had been on another planet for a hundred years. Maurice slipped back easily into his normal routine, John and Margaret looked up their friends and were immediately swallowed up into end of holiday activities but I found it difficult to settle down again.

As always, after a Locum has been in charge, the work pours in from people who have preferred to wait until Maurice's return. Each time I picked up the telephone receiver I heard the same remarks.

'Oh! You're back at last. That's good. I've been waiting to ask Mr Bowring's advice,' or, 'Your Locum said Susie needed a special diet. I'd like to check that with your husband,' and worst of all, the long-winded histories of pets' progress during our absence that made me want to slam down the receiver.

I had had several such calls one day about a week after our return and finally found my self-control slipping when a client, after a long drawn-out description of her dog's health, stated that she wanted Maurice to come that day to see her pet. There was nothing urgent about the case but she said it was impossible for her to bring him to evening Surgery and added, 'I don't mind how late he comes – I never go to bed before midnight.'

Rather sharply, I told her that, even if she didn't mind him working so late, I did, and said that he was so busy that he couldn't do any more calls until the next day.

Pleased with myself for having protected Maurice from such a selfish woman, I expected praise when he returned. But, to my chagrin, he said, after consulting his appointment book, 'Well, as it happens, I can probably fit her in. I've got to go out that way this afternoon and one more call won't make much difference.'

He looked up and met my furious gaze. 'After all the trouble I took to defend you, now you say you can go.'

We settled down to lunch in dignified silence and had nearly finished when the telephone rang. John answered it. 'It's Mrs Mason. She wants you to call this afternoon. Shall I say yes or no?'

Maurice was about to shake his head, when I said sweetly, 'I'm sure you can fit in another call. She's on the way to the one I took.'

Maurice gave in. 'All right. You win. But tell me, why are you so irritable today?'

'It's the telephone, I've had so many long-winded people telling me all the things they can tell you.'

He laughed, 'I've found a good way of dealing with situations like that. Next time we get a suitable subject, I'll show you.'

He was just on the point of leaving when the telephone rang again and, this time, I answered it. To my joy it was a client well known for her talkative nature and, putting my hand over the mouthpiece, I handed the receiver to Maurice.

'Go on,' I urged, 'show me how you deal with her.'

I watched carefully as he listened patiently, took down the necessary details and sighed a little as the monologue went on. Suddenly he began to talk, rather unnecessarily I considered, as he was merely repeating what he had just heard. Then, right in the middle of a phrase, he put his finger down on the button and cut off his client in mid-conversation.

Quietly putting down the receiver, he turned and grinned at my astonished face. 'It always works, they think they've been accidentally cut off because I was talking at the time. Usually, knowing they've given all the necessary information, they don't bother to redial. Mind you, I don't make a habit of doing this. It's only used in a case of real emergency when I have to get away from one of these waffling women . . .' he paused, 'and it's nearly always women who go on like that. Just can't stop talking, I suppose.'

A staunch defender of my sex, I denied this vehemently, but he was out of the house before I had finished my protest, leaving me wondering whether I would have the nerve to cut off a client in the way he had just demonstrated.

I decided that I wasn't ruthless enough and, feeling rather depressed, I resolved to ring up a close friend and have a good heart-to-heart chat. Never mind if clients were trying to get through – Maurice was too busy to attend to them today, anyway. I had poured out my woes and was listening to my friend, when, suddenly, the telephone went dead.

I put down the receiver slowly and stared at it incredulously for a full minute. Surely not? I wasn't being a bore, was I? Well, quite probably I was, but determined to find out, I was about to dial again when I realised that John was standing behind me.

'She's probably got fed-up,' he said, grinning broadly

and looking for a moment just like his father, 'I expect Pop's not the only one who uses that method. I thought you were going on for ever. Sometimes you just can't stop talking.'

Chapter 21

———◆———

A Veterinary Surgeon in Practice on his own has many roles to play. Apart from being a surgeon, he is doctor, anaesthetist, dispenser and often nurse. Into the bargain he must, if he wishes to survive, be a businessman.

This last is, for Maurice, the most difficult part and the one – the only one – he dislikes. 'Doing the Accounts' is guaranteed to make him irritable and when sometimes I try to help, I often find myself in trouble. When I am accused of: (a) distracting him, (b) asking unnecessary questions, (c) not being able to read his – to him – perfectly legible writing, and (d) worst of all – querying his charges, I tend to get somewhat ruffled.

Once a week he transfers details of the calls he has made, which are written in his appointments diary, to filing cards from which he later sends out the accounts. Usually, he does this himself, but when he is very busy, I lend a hand. Being naturally interested in the financial side, I am often surprised and sometimes indignant at what I consider to be ridiculously small charges for a lot of work. This leads to my asking for explanations which, according to Maurice's degree of irritability, are answered or not as the case may be.

On the question of bad debts we are fairly united, agreeing through long experience, on the futility of collecting any fees from certain old hands skilled at the game of avoiding payment. But we fall out when I discover that he has continued to do their work, either because he has gone for the animal's sake or because, in his eternally optimistic fashion, he imagines that they may eventually pay.

A few weeks ago he was called away from writing up the cards to go on a calving case so I took over the task.

He returned, full of satisfaction at a hard job well done and sank into his chair with a sigh of relief. 'How have you got on?' he asked, as I put away the file and shut the appointments book.

I picked up a slip of paper. 'One or two queries,' I said, and he groaned.

'Oh! No! It's all perfectly straightforward. What can't you understand?'

'This for one – on Monday you've got "Call to see Mrs Brown" and then you've crossed her out and written "N.B.G." What exactly does it mean?'

Maurice looked rueful. 'It means, as you ought to know, "No bloody good!" I treated her dog last year, made several calls and finally had to put it to sleep. I've sent out the account at regular intervals and she ignores it completely. I had to do a call in her road so I thought I'd drop in and ask her for my money.' He shrugged his shoulders, 'Hence the N.B.G.'

'Do you mean she wasn't there? Moved house or something?'

'She was there all right. But she pretended not to recognise me and, after I reminded her politely of the times we had met and what she owed me, she put on a wonderful act. Flatly denied she had ever had a dog! Told me I must have made a mistake and remarked lightly that it was quite a coincidence, wasn't it, that she should have the same name but that I had quite obviously got the wrong address.'

'Well, that's lovely,' I said indignantly, 'couldn't you have asked the neighbours?'

'What good would that do? Either they wouldn't want to get involved or I should have to take her to court and it simply isn't worth it for a few pounds.' He chuckled, 'It was almost worth losing the money. She put on a wonderful performance – a born actress.'

I laid that piece of paper down and picked up another. 'Well, now, there's a Mrs Martin. You called several times but you haven't charged anything. Surely that's wrong?'

'No, it's not. Look, why can't you take it for granted that I know what I'm doing?' There was a distinct edge to Maurice's voice.

'Oh! Go on! Do tell me. Are you having a secret affair with a gorgeous blonde? Because, if so, I'd feel in duty bound to give her a few tips in case she has to take my place. You know – how to deal with an irascible Vet when it comes to money matters, wash blood-stained shirts, deal with straw all over newly vacuumed carpets, mend three-cornered jags in trousers from barbed wire, comfort sobbing clients – there's no end to the way in which I could help her . . .'

Maurice got up slowly and went to the dresser. He poured out two drinks and handed one to me. 'There are times when I should like to put a muzzle on you. Mrs Martin, for your information, is about seventy. She is confined to a wheelchair and is extremely lonely. She calls me in quite unnecessarily to see her perfectly healthy cat just to have a chat with someone. We talk about her son who is in prison and she says I cheer her up.'

I choked over my drink. 'Why is her son in prison?'

'He is an ex-public schoolboy who became a solicitor and defrauded his clients, one of whom was his own mother. That's why she has very little money and that's why I don't charge her. But she bears her son no grudge and worries about him constantly. Having been to a similar educational establishment, I am able to assure her that it is a well-known fact that ex-public schoolboys, by virtue of their early training, find it extremely easy to adapt to prison life. It comforts her. She says she feels that the money she and her husband spent on their son's education wasn't entirely wasted after all.'

Maurice reached out for another slip of paper. 'Now what's the next query?'

'Name and address,' I said, 'completely unreadable.'

He looked at it closely, turned it sideways, frowned, turned it the other way, then nodded to himself.

'Plain as a phantom pregnancy. Mrs Ward, Flat two, High Street – you know, that woman who always keeps me waiting if I have to put one of her animals to sleep. She won't let me do it at the Surgery because I haven't the time to spare. She makes me stay there for exactly half-an-hour after I say they are dead then I have to give them another lethal injection. They are ascending, she says, on to a higher plane and their bodies mustn't be disturbed while this is going on otherwise the link will be broken. I don't mind humouring her when it's a dog or a cat but last time it was a guinea pig and I was in a hurry.'

'What happened?' I asked. 'Was the link broken? Is the poor guinea pig going to haunt the flat for ever?'

'I hope not. I left her a syringe filled with water and

she seemed to think everything would be all right.'

'We've certainly got a fair amount of eccentric people in the Practice,' I said.

'Oh, I don't know,' Maurice looked amused, 'we're a bit dotty ourselves. Think of our chickens. We watch them from the moment they're hatched, Margaret and John give them names and turn them into personalities and then, when it comes to eating them, we all suddenly lose our appetites.'

I nodded, remembering the plump cockerels deposited in the deep freeze and recalling the scenes when the query came up, as it always did, 'Is this Napoleon? or Louis?' and the subsequent gloom that hung over the table.

I handed Maurice the last slip of paper. 'Just curiosity on my part, I'd like to know why you've put R.S.P.C.A. underneath this case, with a question mark beside it.'

'Now that was really nasty. I was called to see a cat and when I arrived the woman showed me into a large kitchen. Nothing much wrong – the usual abscess – but when I looked around the room, I saw two cages. In one was a squirrel, darting frantically about, trying desperately to get out and in the other, a thrush, sitting on a perch looking very miserable. The woman saw my look and said proudly, "Aren't they lovely? We picked up the squirrel last week. He had been hit by a car but he could only have been stunned because he soon recovered and the thrush flew into the house and I managed to catch it against the window." I asked, "They're not ill, then?" and she said, "Oh, no. They're perfectly fit and I'm going to keep them. It's interesting for the children." '

'I think that's dreadful,' I said angrily. 'I thought it

was against the law to keep indigenous creatures in cages unless you are treating them for illness and then going to give them their freedom.'

'That's exactly what I told her but she didn't believe me. Said zoos kept them in cages so why shouldn't she? She was treating them kindly, she said. I told her that if she wanted to bring up her children to be completely insensitive to the needs of wild creatures she was going about it the right way and that the only people allowed to do so were zoos and there the animals were kept under very different conditions. I said I'd give her till the next day to set them free and if she didn't, then I'd report her to the R.S.P.C.A. I went round the following day and after a lot more talk she finally agreed and I took the cages outside myself and opened them. She was very huffy and I don't suppose she'll pay me for treating her cat.'

'Marvellous the way people get away with it,' I said, 'shall we try to avoid paying when it comes to the Income Tax demand?'

Maurice stared at me aghast. 'Do you want me to end up in prison?' He paused, 'Come to think of it, it could be quite restful.'

'You never know, they might put you in with old Mrs Martin's son. You could have jolly chats about your school days and she'd be delighted to know that he'd found a suitable friend at last.'

Chapter 22

It was no use, I decided, I would never get back to sleep. Looking at the bedside clock I saw that it was just after five-thirty and Maurice had been out since 4 a.m. on a calving case.

I got out of bed and went to the window where I stood looking out at the garden. It had been a stiflingly hot night but now, with a silvery grey sky and a slight August mist still hovering over the trees, the world was cool and peaceful. The phloxes stood in rose-coloured clumps, soon to be giving out their sweet, powdery scent, the buddleia hung in purple festoons waiting for the butterflies to visit it in fluttering clouds later in the day and roses, asters and tobacco flowers filled the borders.

As I watched, a baby rabbit hopped nonchalantly across the dewy lawn and, although I knew he was heading towards the vegetable garden, I hadn't the heart to break the morning peace by clapping my hands and shooing him away. I leant out of the open window and looked down on the white jasmin covered with heavily scented starlike blossom and drew a deep breath. Heavenly morning, and far too good to waste in sleep. Pulling on my dressing gown, I went downstairs and put on the kettle, then set out the breakfast things all ready to take outside on to the terrace. With a mug of coffee in my hands I went into the garden and sat looking over the fields.

In the distance I saw the shrouded combine harvester

waiting for the men to finish cutting the last of the tall, golden wheat. I was always sorry to see it go. It meant the end of summer and approach of the short, dark days of winter. Sipping my coffee, I reflected on the past year.

It seemed only a few weeks ago that we had been wakened each morning by the cuckoo calling from the woods and all the bird song that fills the air in springtime. Now, in August, the 'silent month', all we heard was the chattering of sparrows and the drowsy cooing of wood pigeons. I remembered the day when we had found cowslips on the brow of the hill and the weeks when one meadow had been dazzlingly brilliant with buttercups and sighed for the quick passing of spring. But every season is beautiful in its own way in the country and autumn and winter have their charms too.

A pheasant came out of the woods and strolled calmly across the field in search of an early breakfast and I was glad that the shooting season was still two months away. Soon, those same birds would become more wary and the clever, cunning ones would escape the guns and live to celebrate the first of February when they could once more flaunt their gorgeous colours in safety.

Just as I was finishing my coffee, I heard the car and as Maurice turned into the drive I got up and went to greet him. He smiled with pleasure as he saw the preparations for breakfast, and soon we were eating our toast and honey in unaccustomed peace.

'I've promised to go down to the Elsdens' to give their dogs the usual check-up this afternoon,' Maurice said. 'You'll come, won't you? It's a nice run and we can take our time as it's my half-day.'

I'd almost forgotten this routine visit but agreed at

once and kept my fingers crossed in case there would have to be a change of plan.

Mr Elsden was a client who had moved away from the Practice a few years ago and had gone to live in a village on the borders of Surrey and Sussex. Instead of going to the local Vet he preferred to remain with Maurice. For a journey like this Maurice usually chose his half-day and Mr Elsden, appreciating the special treatment and being quite comfortably off, sent us each Christmas half-a-dozen bottles of champagne – we gratefully drank his health on birthdays and other special celebrations.

'From what Mr Elsden told me on the telephone last week,' Maurice said thoughtfully, 'I rather think the elder of the two corgis is on the blink. I may have to put him to sleep and, in that case, our visit won't be quite as cheerful as usual. But he and his wife are a very level-headed couple and they won't try to prolong the dog's life for selfish reasons.'

A country drive with Maurice is always a pleasure to me. He sees so many things that I, never very observant, might not notice on my own. Driving along, he will say suddenly, 'Look at that hare out there on the Downs,' or 'Watch that kestrel hovering over the bracken,' and when we pull up to give the dog a run, he points out the tracks of animals and shows the evidence of the hidden life that shares the world with us.

We left soon after lunch and drove in leisurely fashion, avoiding, where possible, busy main roads and choosing the quiet Surrey lanes we know so well. The afternoon was hot and so, before we reached our destination, we stopped by a stream and let the dog out to have a drink. Plunging in, Robert swam around for a few minutes in absolute bliss and then we walked him over the field in order to get dry. Just as we approached a large wood, Maurice halted suddenly.

'Don't move,' he whispered, 'there's a vixen lying out there with cubs. We're downwind of her so if we stand still we can watch.' He pointed to a spot about three hundred yards ahead and then I saw them. It was a pretty sight. The vixen long and thin, lay stretched out in the sun and round and over her three cubs rolled and played like puppies.

'They're about four months old. A late litter, I should think,' said Maurice, 'and much as I dislike foxes I can't help admitting that they look very attractive at that age.'

I watched fascinated as the cubs chased each other, played a kind of tug-of-war with something that was probably a bit of rabbit skin, and stalked butterflies. Every now and then their mother lifted her head watchfully and, satisfied, settled down again for her afternoon nap.

Then, abruptly, Robert came bounding towards us, there was a sharp yap from the vixen and in a flash they all disappeared.

'That was lovely, those cubs were beautiful.'

'All young things are appealing,' said Maurice, as we strolled back to the car, 'but you'll never get me enthusiastic about foxes. They're vicious creatures like stoats and weasels in that they kill for pleasure.'

'You wouldn't want to see them all exterminated, would you?' I asked, thinking of the correspondence I had been reading recently in a newspaper.

'No. Of course not. It depends where they are and in what numbers. A few foxes don't matter; they keep down rats and mice and preserve the balance of nature. And a vixen killing to feed her young is fair enough. But I remember when a fox got into that wood near us where the pheasants are reared. He raced round and round the wire netting of the enclosure where the young ones were until the silly birds panicked and flew over and on to the ground outside. The fox nipped off seventeen heads although it probably only needed one pheasant for food. And the same thing happens if a fox manages to get into a chicken run. They kill for the sheer lust of killing.'

'What about rabies?'

'Well, if it comes to this country and gets into the wild life, foxes will be one of the main carriers.'

'I suppose we will get it eventually, judging from the way it's racing through Europe but I can't see a fox swimming the Channel.'

'It won't come like that. Migrating bats can harbour rabies. Rats from ships can carry it and then, of course, you get these wickedly stupid people who try to smuggle pets into the country. If it comes, it will spread rapidly because the concentration of animals is very high. It will probably get into wild life here if an infected, smuggled dog or cat bites a rat which gets away – rats are pretty tough – and infects other rats when they fight among themselves as they do. Then, they, in turn, bite a fox in self-defence.'

'If a fox were to eat an infected rat would it get rabies?'

'No. It enters the system by the infected saliva getting into the blood stream via an open wound or even a scratch or, of course, by an actual bite. And a dog or a cat with rabies attacks and bites indiscriminately.'

I shuddered. A cloud seemed to have come over the

bright day. 'I suppose all dogs will have to be muzzled then, but what will they do about cats?'

'They will have to be kept in because all stray cats and dogs will be rounded up. The only way to fight it will be by preventive measures – compulsory vaccination for all domestic animals – but you can't vaccinate wild life, so it would then be indigenous.'

We continued our drive and arrived at the Elsdens' house in time for an early tea. The two corgis, Peter and Paul, sat at our feet and looking at the elder one, I saw that Maurice was right. Since our last visit he had become very old.

Mr Elsden saw my face and nodded sadly, 'Yes, I'm afraid Peter has come to the end of his journey.'

His wife's eyes filled with tears and my heart sank as I watched Maurice gently examining the old dog. He looked up when he had finished and sat in silence for a minute. 'Let's see,' he said at last, 'Peter is fourteen, isn't he?'

Mr Elsden nodded, and Maurice went on, 'I'm afraid there's no cure for old age. His kidneys have ceased to function. I did warn you last time and now there's nothing more I can do. He's ninety-eight years old in our terms and he's had a perfect life. Love, care and plenty of exercise.'

It was done quickly and mercifully and as soon as we could, we left, not wishing to intrude on their obvious grief but not before Mr Elsden had told us he would get another corgi to keep Paul company.

When we arrived home the sky, so clear during the day, had clouded and ominous growls of thunder were coming up from the west. The storm broke as we went to bed but tired after our long day, we soon fell asleep.

A few hours later – it seemed only a few minutes – the telephone by our bedside rang and I sat up with a jerk, just in time to hear Maurice say, 'O.K. I'll be right over.' He sighed as he put down the receiver and heaved himself out of bed.

I heard the rain lashing against the window and asked anxiously, 'Who is it? Must you really go?'

Pulling on his trousers, Maurice said, 'The Robertsons' dog,' and it was my turn to sigh because I knew the rest.

It meant a happy release for Kim, gentle, affectionate and highly intelligent, the centre of the Robertsons' world. Twelve years old, the little dog had been dying for a long time. Over a month ago, Maurice had told the Robertsons what they ought to do but they couldn't accept his verdict. Other opinions had been sought and when at last they were convinced, they still could not agree to put Kim to sleep. They loved him too much, they said, to give up so easily. They would fight this thing every inch of the way; they would never give up hope.

In vain, Maurice had tried to make them see that they were not loving Kim enough. They owed him release from his suffering and inevitably there would come a time when they would regret their decision. But they continued to say they would fight on and simply couldn't understand that as far as they were concerned, they were not doing any fighting at all. It was their poor little dog who was struggling with the unconquerable.

For the last week Kim had been very bad and Maurice had begged the Robertsons to let him do what had to be done. Now, at 2 a.m. in the middle of a thunderstorm, they, and Kim, could stand no more.

When Maurice had left the house, I lay awake remembering the many times, and in particular this very afternoon, I had seen him put animals to sleep.

The kind voice soothing their fears, a few comforting caresses and a swift injection that made them feel delightfully drowsy. When in a few minutes they are unconscious, he gives the lethal injection that makes sure they never wake again.

The kindest thing of all, from the animal's point of view, is for the owner to be present, talking in a normal voice and making their pet feel secure and at ease. The Elsdens had been with Peter to the last but I had a feeling that the Robertsons would not be emotionally strong enough to stand the ordeal.

When Maurice returned and climbed wearily into bed, I asked that one question.

'No,' he said tersely, 'they couldn't take it. Their love was the selfish kind.'

I began to ask another question but saw that he had already fallen asleep. A few minutes later he was snoring loudly and, remembering that he had had two disturbed nights running, I stuffed some wads of cotton wool into my ears and fell asleep myself.

Chapter 23

An old school friend of mine had turned up out of nowhere as my old school friends frequently do and was spending a week with us. She seemed to enjoy our unconventional way of life and took particular interest in all veterinary affairs. So, when Maurice said he was going to have an extra long session at the Zoo, she was delighted when he invited us to accompany him.

We were just getting out of the car on our arrival when George came up to greet us. 'Better be careful today, we've had an escape.'

I looked around anxiously and he laughed.

'Only pulling your leg. Actually, it was quite funny. We were standing around having a bit of a break when old Bill looked up and said, "There's something – looks like a pelican – flying over that field. Someone's lost a couple of hundred quid," and sure enough, as it got nearer we could see it quite plainly. There was a bit of a wind blowing and then, as the breeze dropped, down came the bird like a parachute. Landed on the pond over there.' He chortled, 'It was one of ours.'

'I thought they had their wings clipped,' I said. 'How on earth did it take off?'

'They only have one clipped and, sometimes, if they spread them out, a strong wind will make them rise like a kite. They can only soar, of course, and once the wind drops all they can do is to control their rate of descent with a few flaps. No harm done and I daresay it makes a nice change for the bird.'

'Do you get many real escapes?' Elizabeth asked.

George shook his head. 'No. We're very careful. But, naturally, things happen occasionally.' He turned to Maurice, 'Remember old Ted? The brown Russian bear?'

'Good Lord, yes!' Maurice said, then seeing that Elizabeth was fascinated, he went on, 'It was some time ago, before we had the Cap-Chur gun and it was early in the morning before the public had arrived. When I got there, I found keepers guarding every exit with rifles and everybody in a great state. Ted's cage door had been left slightly open and he'd pulled at it with his sharp claws and suddenly found himself outside. He then began to amble around the grounds, causing great consternation because bears are difficult to handle on account of their uncertain temperament. Brown bears aren't as vicious as their cousins, the Polar bears, but they never change their expression so it's impossible to know whether they're feeling nasty or not.'

'He wouldn't co-operate though, would he?' George said. 'We were all trying to shoo him back towards his cage but he didn't want to know. As soon as anyone approached, he roared and made a half-hearted rush at them, not exactly attacking but just warning them to keep their distance. It went on for some time and we were all trying to work out some method of outwitting him when he suddenly got bored with it all, strolled back to his cage and flopped down with a sigh of relief.'

As we were passing the monkey walk, Elizabeth pointed to the inmates and asked George, 'What about those? Do they get out at all?'

'Not really. The babies sometimes wriggle through the

bars, but they never go far and at the first sign of danger, they rush back in again. Their parents don't seem to worry but they keep an eye on them rather like humans when their children are playing on the beach. Some of the small adult monkeys get out by squeezing through small gaps they make in the wire. We have to block these up pretty quickly or the rest of the colony would come pouring out. But these small ones don't wander far either. They usually play around in the trees and come back to be caught when they get hungry.'

'Now we're here,' said Maurice, 'we might as well begin with the monkeys . . . Any new arrivals?'

George pointed, 'Yes. That little Rhesus monkey. She had her baby yesterday and everything seems normal.'

We could just see the tiny head and bright eyes peeping from its mother's fur. It clung to her tightly whilst she wandered around unconcernedly eating fruit. Then, settling down into a corner, she began to feed it, looking across at us with indifference, but at her nestling baby with obvious love and pride.

Maurice went on, 'Luckily, help is very seldom needed at these births. Usually all we have to do is to make sure that the mother is all right and that there is plenty of milk for the baby, with no mastitis or other infection.'

'I suppose on the whole,' said Elizabeth, 'monkeys are fairly tough.'

'Oh, no. You're thinking of baboons. Monkeys are very delicate and subject to infections of all kinds. They fight a lot and the bites and cuts almost always turn septic so constant watch must be kept. They're also very subject to colds and chest complaints but it's terribly difficult to treat a baby when it gets ill. The mother will never allow you to examine it and, whilst she's feeding it herself, it's impossible to separate them so one must concentrate on prevention. We've found the best way to avoid bronchial infections is to keep them in the open all the year round, with heated dens into which they can go at night.'

'That little fellow over there has got a bite,' said George. 'He was in a fight yesterday. See, there it is — on his right shoulder.'

Maurice went to examine it more closely. 'Hmm. Looks a bit nasty. I think you'd better isolate him for a couple of days and put this antibiotic in his drinking water. You can't keep him on his own much longer than that, can you, or the troop won't accept him when he goes back.'

We moved on to the ape house and Maurice explained, 'Now here, you see, it's quite different. Apes, as opposed to monkeys, can't stand cold at all. In the winter, they have to be kept indoors and, as far as it is possible, away from direct contact with humans because they catch our infections easily.'

'Look at Monty,' said George, 'he seems to be enjoying life.'

The young chimpanzee was wrestling and romping with his mate and, as I watched, I remembered the difficulties that had arisen when Monty first arrived at the Zoo with his sister, Milly. Two young chimpanzees had been asked for, round about two years old. But something went wrong and, instead, the Zoo received two pathetic little babies of well under a year.

I asked George to tell me the story.

'Well, they were frightened out of their wits, poor little

things,' George began, 'They both had streaming colds and they clung to each other and chattered in terror at anyone's approach. They were really too young to leave their mother so they had to be fed from bottles and this was the only comfort they would accept from us. Monty's cold got better but Milly developed pneumonia and died, and poor Monty was heartbroken. He sat in the cage, rocking himself backwards and forwards in utter misery and we decided we couldn't leave him like that. So we put nappies on him and took him into the office. He immediately perked up and, before long, he was having the time of his life. Into everything – he helped himself to biscuits and had all kinds of snacks – he became a real little pickle.'

Maurice laughed, 'I remember when I used to come in, he'd leap up on to the top of the cupboard and then take a flying jump right on to my shoulders.'

George continued, 'We thought we'd never get him used to a cage again but, when we found him a playmate, he was delighted and all was well.'

'Now here's Giles,' said Maurice, pointing to a fully-grown chimpanzee who stood staring at him suspiciously. 'He's never quite trusted me since that time when we were trying to get a chain off his neck. It dated from the days when he had been safe to handle and, unfortunately, when he came here, it hadn't been removed and it was already much too tight. First of all we tried tranquillisers but Giles wasn't having anything like that and when I handed him a "doctored" grape, he looked me straight in the eye and threw it back in my face. It was just at the time we had got the Cap-Chur gun so we decided to try it out on him. We must have looked very conspiratorial because he immediately shot up to the top of his cage and hung there, barking and glaring at us. Chimps hate anything being pointed at them and their immediate reaction is to chatter and jump around which doesn't help. We couldn't have a moving target because the dart must be fired into a thick muscle such as the haunch. So George distracted him by pretending to search for a tit-bit in his pocket and soon he grew still and interested and I managed to fire a full anaesthetic plop into his behind. He whipped his hand down to where it stung but he didn't realise what had happened though he turned and glared at me for a few seconds. Then, suddenly, there he was – flat out on the floor of his cage. We got the chain off quickly, wrapped him up warmly and he came round normally. But he still doesn't trust me.'

We left the apes and went round to the animals living in large paddocks and Maurice remarked, 'I'm always glad to see wild creatures living in as much space as possible but, even then, you can't get away from the fact that there are lots of problems caused by keeping them in captivity. There was a good example – or rather a bad one – with the zebras.'

'They look perfectly happy,' said Elizabeth, 'and they've certainly got plenty of room.'

'Yes, but in the wild state, zebras roam in large herds and although the males have no paternal instincts, they accept additions to their numbers as a natural state of affairs. Freddy and Freda here had lived in a confined space for so long – some ten years in fact – that when Freda unexpectedly had a foal, the male violently resented another zebra, however small, entering his territory.'

George went on, 'We never suspected she was pregnant after all that time but, one day, there was a tremendous commotion in the paddock. You could hear the squeals all over the Zoo. When we rushed over to them we were absolutely amazed to see that Freda had had a foal which was being fiercely attacked by its father. We turned hoses on to them and managed to drive Freddy into a separate enclosure. He calmed down then and Freda's baby wasn't severely injured so he lived happily with his mother for some months. We all thought that his father, who was on the other side of the fence had accepted the situation, but we were wrong. One day, Freddy, in a sudden, blind fury, jumped at the fence which partially collapsed and he got through. Then he attacked the foal again. Freda defended it with all her strength but, as the parents stood back to back, lashing out at each other, the poor little foal got kicked by both. At last we got them separated but, by then, the young one was so badly injured that it had to be put down. Freda was very upset, kept whinnying for her baby all the time, so, rather nervously, we let her mate return to her and they settled down again at once.'

'That was over three years ago,' said Maurice, 'but the gestation period is twelve months so we're always on the alert now in case she gets pregnant again.'

As we walked along, Elizabeth said, 'Of course, I realise that you couldn't dart the zebras in the middle of their fight, but the dart gun must have made a big difference to you when it comes to dealing with all these animals.'

'It certainly has. I think, as a Vet, my life expectancy is much greater now. However, you can't use it in many cases of illness because a dose of anaesthetic would probably finish the animal off. Pneumonia, for instance. But it's useful for moving large animals around, though even then it's very easy to make mistakes. I'll never forget the time we had with the old tiger, Zaba. He was a very tough customer indeed and he had to be moved from a cage to an open-air compound. We simply couldn't lure or drive him into a travel box so I said I'd anaesthetise him. We had a general discussion on his weight and as nobody was really sure we compromised on four hundred pounds and I calculated the dose on that basis. I shot in the dart but, even after a quarter of an hour, Zaba showed no signs of it having affected him at all. I was sure the dart had gone in properly so, thinking I had underestimated his weight, I decided to add another dose and made it up for an additional hundred pounds. He went down quickly this time and we were able to drag him into the box and move him into the compound. But hours later he was still unconscious. I began to get worried and injected an antidote. His respiration and heart beats improved slightly but it was several days before he was fully recovered. It was a pretty near thing. Looking back, I think that some of the anaesthetic must have gone into an area of fat over the muscle, from which it would be only slowly absorbed into the blood stream. Zaba probably had a fatty liver too, due to his life of good food and not much exercise and that would account for the slowness of his recovery. So, you see, the gun is not the complete answer to our problems. There's so often an unknown factor to upset calculations.'

We visited more animals. Lions, tigers, elephants and giraffes and I began to wonder whether Elizabeth would not soon become bored. But she seemed to find it fascinating and listened eagerly to the stories Maurice and George exchanged. Some of them were old history to me so I wandered away to look at a few more unusual inhabitants. Suddenly, I came across what seemed to me to be a most extraordinary creature. It was rather like an ostrich, not as large but with the oddest-looking neck. The skin was bright blue with large, fleshy appendages hanging from the throat. I stood gazing at it and soon Maurice and the others joined me.

'It's a male cassowary,' George informed us, 'and he and his mate have just hatched a chick. We're very pleased because it's a rare occurrence in this country. The female laid three eggs – two didn't hatch – and that's her job done. She shows no further interest – it's father's work from then on. He sits on the eggs and looks after them entirely. See – there's the baby.'

The little brown bird was about ten inches long with dark stripes running down its back and, as we stared at it, George said, 'They don't stand upright at first but walk in that peculiar way with their necks stretched right out in a straight line. It's a strange bird.'

As we peered over the fence, the cock bird came forward aggressively and we moved quickly back in order to avoid being pecked in the face.

'Cassius is very protective, but Clara couldn't care less. She's in the next compound. Seems unusual, doesn't it?'

Elizabeth laughed, 'I think it's rather a good idea. After all, she had to produce the eggs. It's a perfect example of sex equality.'

'By the way,' George added, 'the ostrich over here – the one that was lame – seems O.K. now. Shall we stop the medicine?'

The great bird was lying down at the end of his paddock and Maurice said he'd just like to observe its walk. Opening the gate, he went in. The ostrich got up quickly and moved away whilst Maurice stood watching him carefully.

'Yes,' he said, as he came back to us, 'he's perfectly all right again. The cortico steroid has done the trick.'

Then, as he took a final look at the bird, he began to chuckle, 'Watch this, it's most interesting if rather indelicate.'

The ostrich, with his back towards us was passing rather loose droppings and as soon as he had finished, Maurice said, 'Now see what Nature has given him – an automatic bottom wiper.'

To our amusement we saw what seemed to be a long tongue emerge from its back passage, pass quickly over the surface like a windscreen wiper and vanish inside again.

When we had recovered from our hilarity, Maurice said, 'I think that's quite a good note on which to end our tour but I must go into the quarantine quarters to check on the animals there before we leave.'

We waited outside and when he came out again I asked him what was in there that day.

'Let's see,' he consulted his list, 'four Barbary apes, two agoutis, two pacas – strange creatures with white blotches all over them and liable to bite. I have to report on them every week for six months to the Ministry of Agriculture.'

'What are you looking for? Rabies?'

'Yes, mainly. I look for listlessness, restlessness, anything abnormal. If any of them should die and I suspect

172

rabies then I have to send the creature's head to the Ministry for examination. The regulations are very strict and quite rightly.' Maurice turned to George, 'By the way, that dung sample from the camel that I sent to the laboratory has come back positive. So, if you'll get some men to help hold it, I'll inject it tomorrow. I'll come in early before the visitors arrive and then we can dart that lion and see if I can do something about those cuts he's got on his pad. That's the lot for today, isn't it?'

I was thankful. For once I had had my fill of the Zoo and all I wanted was to get away from animals and sit down to a large cup of coffee.

I looked at Elizabeth and she smiled back at me, then turned to Maurice. 'Next time I feel ill I think I'll call in my Vet,' she said.

'Humans aren't my field. Give me animals every time. But you know what they say – when anything has been "vetted" it's O.K. but when it's been "doctored" that's another story!'

Chapter 24

'What do you think is the matter with him?' asked th
agitated voice at the other end of the telephone. 'He'
shivering and miserable and when I pick him up he goe
all rigid. I don't know what to do.'

'I should just keep him warm and quiet,' I said, 'M
Bowring will be along as soon as possible – probabl
within the hour.'

'Oh, dear! So I've got to wait. That's Mrs Bowring
isn't it? I expect you can help me. It isn't like my Benj
to act like this. Do you think he's going to have a fit o
something? Or could it be his heart?'

'Honestly, I don't know, I'm not a Veterinary Surgeon
But I shouldn't worry too much if I were you. It'
probably not serious.'

'You don't think so? Oh, that's good. I felt sure you'
know.' There was a long pause, 'But he's got such a sac
look in his little eyes and – oh, dear! he's shivering again
Do you think he's got pneumonia?'

'No,' I said firmly, 'I don't. I expect it's just a chill.'

'A chill! But that could lead to pneumonia, couldn'
it? You will tell your husband it's urgent, won't you? M
Benjy with pneumonia, oh, my goodness!'

Cursing myself inwardly, I chose my words carefully
'Please don't get so worried, Mrs Brown. I suggested a
chill' (and how I wish I hadn't) 'but I don't know any
more than you do. I must pass your message on straight

174

way so I'll ring off now and my husband will soon be with you.'

I put down the receiver and drew a long breath. After all these years I should know better than to fall into that trap. Hurriedly, I rang some places where Maurice was due to call and went back to my housework, mentally preparing my defence in case Mrs Brown greeted Maurice with the words 'Your wife thinks Benjy has pneumonia.'

It was always the same, I reflected ruefully. The agitated clients who thought I knew as much as the Vet, were the bane of my life. Mrs Brown's husband was an architect but that was no reason to suppose that Mrs Brown could draw up the plans for a new Town Hall so why should she think I knew what was wrong with her dog? Knowing Mrs Brown, I had a pretty shrewd idea that Benjy's symptoms were greatly exaggerated and it probably was just a chill but I ought to have learnt by now that it was no use talking as one lay person to another. Without any justification whatsoever, people tended to take my comments on their pets as being deep and knowledgeable.

Sometimes it was highly embarrassing. I remember once, at a friend's house, commenting on the amusing way her little dog held his head, and the next thing I knew she had brought it into the Surgery and told Maurice that she suspected brain damage. In answer to Maurice's astonished query, she said, 'Your wife saw something at once and that was enough for me.'

Maurice's forcible remarks to me afterwards did nothing to soothe my indignation and I resolved, in future, to praise every animal I met. But this didn't work either because, on another occasion, I patted and admired a very well covered spaniel and the owner glared at me and said, 'Your husband says he's much too fat and in danger of heart disease.'

As far as I could see, unless I pretended to have no interest in animals at all, there was no avoiding such situations. What would happen, I wondered, if, when people began asking my advice as to what to do about Fido's habit of catching and eating flies or Sooty's mania for best red salmon, I replied, 'Don't ask me. I couldn't care less about animals'? That would be good for the Practice, wouldn't it? I could just hear the whispers: 'He's a good Vet but she's horrible. Hates animals, you know.'

But the temptation to diagnose is an unforgivable sin in a Vet's family and the quite unjustified conviction that one knows it all must be eradicated early on. I smiled to myself as I recalled how John, when small, was in the habit, as we found to our cost, of telling his friends that their guinea pigs, hamsters or pet mice were in dire need of an operation (unspecified) in order to save their lives and, when found out, protested that he was only trying to 'help Daddy get lots of work'. And Margaret had had a phase of wandering into the Waiting Room and causing alarm and despondency by her tearful pity for the patients. 'Your poor doggie looks very ill, doesn't he?' she would say when the astonished owner was only bringing it in to have its toe-nails cut.

We have, however, learnt discretion over the years and I was the only one who occasionally slipped up as I had done this morning. But that was nothing very important. In my early days as a Vet's wife, flushed with reflected glory, I thought I knew it all. Until the day when an old

176

farmer rang to tell me that one of his cows had 'pushed her calf bed out' and asked that Maurice should come at once. Thinking that this was merely a neurotic animal engaged in throwing the straw around, I felt that the farmer was being unnecessarily demanding and as Maurice was very busy, I didn't bother to pass on the message. I told him at lunch time, laughing merrily over such a foolish tale, only to have my breath taken away by the words, 'For God's sake, that means a prolapse of the uterus and it's urgent!' and I was left staring at the remains of a half-eaten meal.

It was then that I began to realise how little I really knew. My education has progressed and now, after many mistakes, I am usually able to sort out the messages in order of priority.

When it comes to our own animals however, I find being the Vet's wife is hard going. How many times have I heard myself muttering things about cobblers' children always being the worst shod and being informed that 'There is absolutely nothing wrong with the dog – you're just imagining symptoms,' and, when I persist have been asked, 'Well, would you like to call in another Vet?' Sometimes, very rarely I admit, I have been right in noticing the onset of an illness but then I learn that the necessary treatment has already been given and that I haven't been told because I would only worry needlessly.

My reflections were suddenly interrupted by a loud peal from the door bell and, hurriedly pulling myself together, I went to answer it. A woman, holding a small dog in her arms, said, 'He's hurt his paw. Cut the pad badly and it's bleeding terribly. Is the Vet in?'

I shook my head. 'I'm sorry. My husband is out on

calls but if you'll come into the Surgery I'll bandage th
paw up for you.'

When the dog was on the table I saw that the cut wa
only slight but, as always in these cases, it was bleedin
profusely.

'Makes me feel quite bad,' said the woman, 'but
suppose you're used to these things. You'd know as muc
as the Vet I should think.'

'I certainly don't. What does your husband do?'

'Ron? Oh, he's a mechanic in a garage.'

'So you know all about car engines, then,' I said, an
she stared at me in astonishment.

'I'm sorry, I was only joking. Now, if you'll hold th
dog still, I'll tie this big wad of cotton wool round hi
foot, then I'll bandage it up.'

When that was done I took a cut-down sock kept for th
purpose, placed the dog's foot inside and tied it on firmly

'There,' I said, 'the bleeding will soon stop and h
won't be able to pull off the bandage.'

Satisfied, the woman went away, after promising t
bring her dog in to the evening Surgery for Maurice t
check and, as I shut the door behind her, I gave mysel
a mental pat on the back.

Elementary, of course, but I knew I had done the righ
thing. I must be nearly as good as a – no, not a Vet –
perhaps a veterinary nurse. Well, that was one step u
the ladder, anyway.

Chapter 25

The house was filled with the pounding of electric guitars,
record players poured out pop music and the throb of
the washing-machine added to the general confusion.
Every room seemed to be filled with teenagers, there were
perpetual cries for food and the fridge and the freezer
were in constant need of replenishment.

The long school holidays were nearing their end and so,
I felt, was I.

The battle for the telephone had finally been won by
me when I discovered John, carried away no doubt by
the admiration of his friends, giving flippant answers to
clients. Forbidden to answer any more calls, they all
crowded round every time I picked up the receiver in
case it should be Eddie, Dave, Susan, Penny or whoever
was not there at the moment.

Doggedly I waded through the washing and ironing
and longed for the fast approaching day when school and
homework would make for comparative peace once more.

The telephone rang yet again and to cries of 'Perhaps
that's Debbie – no, I expect it will be James' I went to
answer it while half-a-dozen boys and girls crowded round.

'Oh, hello Mrs Hammond,' I said, 'no, he's not here
at the moment. May I take a message?'

'It's about Evelyn, my goat. There's something wrong
with him. His milk has stopped.'

'Did you say "he"? A male goat giving milk? Surely . . .'

I looked round hastily at the intent faces breaking into

wide grins and waved them away.

'I must have mistaken what you said,' I said apologetically, 'I thought you said "he" but, of course, the name should have told me. You mean your nanny goat isn't giving milk.'

'No, I don't. And "Evelyn" is a name that applies to boys and girls. Not that Evelyn is a boy or a girl come to that. You must have heard all about him – her – oh, dear you've got me all muddled. Anyway, Evelyn's milk has stopped for some reason or other and I want Mr Bowring to come over.'

Mrs Hammond's voice was loud and clear but there was silence all round me so, to make sure the teenagers had gone, I half-turned, only to find them gazing at me in hopeful expectation of more information on this enthralling aspect of the facts of life.

'Are you there? I think this line is bad so I'll speak loudly,' Mrs Hammond's voice became even more penetrating, and there was a sort of concerted rush as my youthful listeners hemmed me in despite my frantic signals. 'Evelyn served, you know – mated, two nanny goats that were brought here yesterday but, when I went to milk him this morning, there wasn't a drop. I usually get about a pint a day.'

'I don't quite understand,' I said weakly, 'but I'll get my husband to come over as soon as possible.'

A burst of hearty laughter came through the receiver. 'You don't understand? Oh, I see! Of course, I should have realised. Evelyn is a hermaphrodite – you know – male and female at the same time. Mr Bowring knows all about him. He's a great pet. Evelyn, I mean, not your husband. Not that he isn't a pet, too, but – goodness

I'm getting all tied up. Tied up – yes – that's right. I've got Evelyn tied up waiting for Mr Bowring so I hope he won't be long. I expect he'll put Evelyn right in no time – well, as right as he'll – she'll – ever be. Ha! Ha!'

I put down the receiver slowly and threaded my way through the sea of grinning faces. As I went into the kitchen, a great roar of conversation burst out behind me and glancing back as I closed the door, I saw my audience falling about with merriment.

'Evelyn,' I said to myself, preparing a much needed cup of coffee, 'he serves the nanny goats and gives a pint of milk a day. Now I've heard everything.'

My stunned thoughts were interrupted by the re-opening of the kitchen door. John, spokesman for the group behind him, said, 'We'd like to know more about Evelyn. Will you get Pop to tell us the story when he comes back? It would be awfully interesting for Biology.'

I looked at their faces, red with suppressed mirth. I suppose you want to take the mickey out of your unfortunate Biology master,' and began to laugh as they tried to put on a show of earnest denial.

However, I had to agree that, scientifically speaking, it was of interest and promised to give them Evelyn's history when Maurice had enlightened me.

I handed him the message when he came home and he looked up and grinned.

'Why haven't you told me about Evelyn?' I asked indignantly. 'I made a perfect fool of myself on the telephone this morning. I began to think I was going mad under the strain of coping with school holidays.'

He laughed. 'The subject never seemed to arise.'

'Well, now it has. So will you explain? I've got to give

full details to John. He wants to hold the Biology clas
spell-bound.'

'There's no real explanation. No one knows why thes
things happen. It's a mix-up of hormones. It isn't un
common in domestic animals and it's often seen in goats
Evelyn is quite adequate as a male and is a good stu
goat. As for the milk, well it must be taken away otherwis
he would develop mastitis.'

'Does Mrs Hammond actually drink it?'

'Why not? Goat's milk is very good though it has
strong flavour. It makes fine yoghurt too. Mrs Hammon
has got the best of both worlds in Evelyn.'

I passed on this information to John who rushed off t
tell his friends, hoping aloud that there would be a
Evelyn among the new boys next term. Sending up
silent prayer for any such unlucky youth, I returned to m
work.

The chaos of holiday time continued. Shopping ex
peditions were made, the usual arguments took plac
with Margaret with regard to the length of her ne
school skirt and every time the telephone rang, th
teenagers gathered round hopefully.

By the end of the last week I was growing irritable an
tired.

'Cheer up,' said Maurice, leaving to go out on calls
'you'll soon be back to normal and then you'll be able t
take a little interest in me.'

I was in no mood for such flippancy. 'It's all right fo
you, you can be out all day and only come home whe
things have quietened down. Sometimes I wish I were
man.'

Maurice made for the door. 'I'm very glad you aren't.

That lunch time he came home early, carrying a bottle wrapped around with brown paper. 'There you are.' He put it on the table, 'With grateful thanks from Evelyn.'

I stared distrustfully at the goat's milk. 'Ugh! How revolting. I couldn't possibly drink that.' A thought occurred to me, 'Besides, you don't know what it could do. It might make me change sex or something.'

'Well, isn't that just what you wanted this morning? I seem to remember you expressing a wish to be a man.'

'I've changed my mind, in any case, it probably wouldn't make a thorough job of it and I might turn out like Evelyn.'

'I tell you what,' Maurice suggested, 'we'll offer it to John and his friends. They ought to try it in the interests of science.' There was great hilarity but, although Maurice assured them that the milk was fit to drink, it got a very poor reception.

But Robert, the dog, enjoyed it immensely and in spite of dire prophecies from the teenagers, we did not have to change his name to 'Roberta'.

Chapter 26

It was Sunday and Margaret, John and I were having late breakfast. Maurice was still in bed and I was deter mined that he should stay there as long as possible. He had been called out during the night to a difficult calving cas from which he returned about four-thirty, exhausted and almost asleep on his feet. Added to this, he was suffering from a heavy cold, so I was in a fighting mood, resolved that no one would get him out today for anything tha was not really urgent.

Cunningly, I had pressed down the little button on the extension telephone by his bed so that he would not be awakened by the bell and he was sleeping so deeply tha I knew he would never hear it ring downstairs.

I only hoped we would not get any calls from thos clients known to us as 'Sunday regulars'. These are over dedicated animal lovers who, labouring under the illusion that Vets are just longing to forgo their meals or jump out of bed, even a sick bed, to investigate any triviality decide that their pets are not quite one hundred per cen and must be seen at once. They are also the ones who take the longest time to pay their bills and are frequently indignant when charged extra for Sunday work.

I was just beginning to hope that today would be uneventful when the telephone rang.

'Mrs Pullen here,' said a mournful voice, and I closed my eyes in despair, waiting for the tale of woe that was this client's speciality. A well-meaning but rather stupid woman, she kept a collection of creatures that, somehow or other, never seemed to thrive. Her garden was overrun with other people's rejects. She always bought the weakest puppies, her children's guinea pigs developed skin infections and the chickens succumbed to mysterious diseases.

'It's Nellie, my white hen,' she said, 'she's been egg-bound since yesterday. Will you ask Mr Bowring to come at once, please?'

I drew a long breath and then told her that Maurice was not available.

'But I want him now,' she said plaintively, 'it can't possibly wait until tomorrow.'

'I'm sorry, but why not try to ease the egg out your-self? If you lubricate around the exit area that should help.'

There was a shocked silence, then she said, 'I could never do that. I'm sure Mr Bowring would come if you would let me speak to him. Is he in?'

'Yes, he is,' I said rather sharply, 'but he was out for most of the night and he has a very bad cold. I want him to stay in bed if possible.'

'But what about my poor Nellie? Something must be done. It probably won't take very long.'

'I think you had better try to get another Veterinary Surgeon, there are several very good ones around here. Would you like me to give you their numbers?'

'No thank you, I want Mr Bowring. Perhaps, if I rang later on he might be able to come, though I'm sure poor Nellie can't go on much longer like this. She's always getting egg-bound and Mr Bowring said last time that he didn't think she ought to be allowed to continue.'

185

'Well, there you are, that's your answer.'

There was another long silence. 'What exactly do you mean, Mrs Bowring?' she asked warily.

I threw all caution to the winds. 'Your best plan is to put Nellie out of her misery and have boiled chicken for dinner tomorrow.'

There was a click as Mrs Pullen put down the receiver and I sank, trembling, into an armchair.

For heaven's sake! What had I done? Then, slowly, an enormous glow of satisfaction swept over me, and I decided that it was well worth it even if Mrs Pullen complained about me to everyone she knew. But suddenly I felt a chill. What about poor wretched Nellie? For the next hour I was haunted by the thought of the unhappy hen and when the telephone rang again and I heard the mournful voice once more I began to stammer out some kind of apology.

'Oh! But you were perfectly right, Mrs Bowring, I've taken your advice. Nellie had to go.' Mrs Pullen sounded quite friendly.

'You -- you mean . . .?'

'Yes. My neighbour came in and did what was necessary. It was very quick. I thought I'd better tell you in case Mr Bowring decided to come out later on.'

I felt an insane desire to ask whether she was going to take the rest of my advice but restrained myself in time.

'I'm so glad,' I said weakly, 'I'm sure it was for the best.'

'Yes, it was. But I don't think I can do the other thing you suggested.'

'The other thing?'

'You suggested that I should -- I hardly like to say it --

"boil her and have her for dinner". I don't think that's a very nice idea.'

'No. No, of course not,' I said hastily, 'it wasn't meant to be taken seriously. It was just a joke – well, not a joke, exactly, but . . .' I stopped. I was getting incoherent.

'So I thought you'd like to know that my neighbour has buried her at the end of the garden. Under the apple tree and near the rabbit hutches.'

'Oh! that's nice,' I said, as steadily as I could, 'very nice indeed.'

'I'm glad you think so. Anyway, will you tell Mr Bowring that I think Fenella the rabbit is going to have her babies soon, so that he can be on the alert?'

'I'll tell him,' I promised, 'I'll tell him everything.'

Maurice came down at lunch time feeling much better and smiled approvingly at my rather high-handed treatment of his client. 'Perhaps we'll be able to cross her off the list of "Sunday regulars", she'll be so scared of you that she'll prefer to ring during Surgery hours.'

'Let's hope so,' I said. 'There goes that damn telephone again. I'll take it.'

'I don't think you know me, I got your number from the exchange. My dog has had an accident and his back legs seem to be paralysed. Could the Vet come at once, please?'

While he was giving his address, I considered how best to deal with this emergency. If I told Maurice, he would go out so I said, 'It will be much easier to examine the dog if you can bring it here to the Surgery. It may need an anaesthetic.'

In about ten minutes a low slung sports car drew up outside and a good-looking young man brought in a little fox terrier. As soon as we put him on to the table in the Surgery, the dog lifted his head and began to howl pathetically. Catching a glimpse of his owner's face I saw that he was going alarmingly pale.

'Here,' I said, putting a chair under him. 'You look as though you're suffering from shock.'

'I am, I ran Dandy over myself. I was backing out of the garage and didn't see him in the drive. I left my mother practically in hysterics. Is he very bad?'

Maurice looked up from his examination. 'I thought you said his back legs were paralysed? There are no signs of it now. But he's pretty badly bruised. Don't worry. When a dog howls like that there's not much wrong. He's had a very lucky escape.'

The young man said nothing and I turned just in time to see him slump on to the floor.

Maurice put the dog in a basket and attended to his overwrought client and the little terrier howled louder than ever. Suddenly getting out of the basket he walked across the room and squatted in the middle of the floor where he proceeded to pass a motion. Then he went back to his basket and settled down quietly.

When, at last, he and his embarrassed master had left, we cleaned up the mess and Maurice grinned at me as he saw the look on my face. 'Pleasant little interlude in the middle of Sunday lunch.'

Two more people rang in the afternoon but we managed to put them off till the next day, and then we settled down for the evening.

On Monday morning a client rang just before breakfast and Maurice took the call. He came back looking annoyed. 'The other extreme, the dog has just died and I could have saved it if the owner had rung me yesterday. But they said they didn't like to disturb me on a Sunday.'

I frowned. 'Isn't it strange, some people are selfish and some are unselfish and both kinds can be equally foolish.'

'They're the ones who have no common sense,' said Maurice.

When he had gone, I sat for a while, deep in thought. It was surprising how many folk, probably very capable, very intelligent folk, were utterly stupid when it came to dealing with animals.

Come to think of it, I wasn't particularly bright myself. If I were not married to a Vet and an animal belonging to me seemed a bit off colour on a Sunday, what would I do? Recalling the way I invariably panic when our dog seems unwell, I nodded my head slowly. I had a strong suspicion that I might come into the same category as Mrs Pullen and her white hen.

Chapter 27

The farmhouse kitchen door was wide open and as we pulled into the yard I could see old Mrs Bond sitting at the table gazing across the fields. At first, she seemed almost unaware of our arrival and I felt a sharp pang of pity as I remembered that, in a few days' time, she would have exchanged that lovely view for the confining walls of a small bungalow or flat.

When we got out of the car and walked across the yard, she rose slowly and came to greet us. 'It was nice of you to come, I hope you've time for a cup of tea.'

'We'd love one,' I said, and Maurice, who had planned this visit carefully, added, 'I've nothing urgent on this afternoon so there's no need to watch the clock.'

Mrs Bond seemed glad of the chance to do something and she quickly arranged the cups and saucers and produced a home-made cake.

It was not a happy occasion. Some months ago old Mr Bond had died after a short illness and now with the farm already sold, Mrs Bond was making ready to leave. She had told Maurice that she was going to live with her sister and unable to take the dog and two cats with her, she wanted him to put them to sleep. It was at his suggestion that I had come along with him in case I could give any comfort to the old lady but, to my relief, she seemed calm and resigned. She talked of her husband with quiet restraint and I marvelled at her patient acceptance of sorrow.

'I was thinking,' she said, as she poured the tea, 'of all the years I've looked out at these fields and enjoyed watching them change with the seasons. But now that Matthew has gone, it only makes me sad, so it's much better that I should go right away. In any case, I couldn't farm here on my own and the two boys are both in Canada. I'm going to live with my sister down by the sea.'

'That will be a complete contrast,' I said, and she nodded.

'Yes. I think it's better that way. My sister spent all her time with our parents on our father's farm and, when they died, she said she could never bear to box herself up in a road with only houses to look at so she took this flat overlooking the sea and, that way, she has space in front of her which can never be built up.'

It was an idea that had never occurred to me but, as I visualised the sea in its many moods, with ships and sea birds to watch, I realised she was right. The gales of winter would cause no alarm to anyone who had lived in this exposed, solitary farmhouse and however small the flat, she would never feel hemmed in with that vast expanse outside the windows.

Maurice asked gently, 'I suppose the flat isn't big enough for you to take your dog and cats?'

She shook her head slowly, 'That's not why I'm having them put to sleep. My sister is quite willing for me to take them but I don't think it would be kind. They're all rather old and Jack, the dog, went everywhere with my husband – he misses him terribly – and the cats have had a wild, free life. It wouldn't be fair to shut them up and I can't walk as I used to. I think it would be cruel to uproot them at their age.'

Maurice nodded in approval. 'You're absolutely right—I would do the same in your circumstances.'

'I've left it almost till the last minute, but as I'm moving out tomorrow, I'm afraid the time has come.'

I saw her hand tremble slightly as she refilled Maurice's cup. 'I'll call them in soon, I'd like them to have a nice meal first.'

Suddenly, as I looked at the bowls of food standing under the sink, I felt repelled. It seemed so horribly cold blooded. I wondered what I would have done under the same conditions but my imagination failed me and I could only sit waiting apprehensively for the moment when Mrs Bond would call in the animals. I had expected to have to give comfort but now I began to wish I had never come.

My thoughts must have shown in my face because Mrs Bond reached across and touched my hand. 'It's hard, I know, my dear, but when you're my age you'll come to realise that a happy death in your own surroundings is infinitely better than being taken away from all you love best and my animals haven't got much longer to live anyway.'

It was then that I understood the pain underneath her calm acceptance of events and I felt that, although she was trying to concentrate on the attractions of life by the sea, she would never really recover from the wrench of leaving her beloved farm.

We finished our tea and then Mrs Bond got up. 'Now, my dear,' she said to me, 'I think it would be a good idea if you took a stroll round the garden while I stay here with your husband.'

I was only too glad to do as she suggested and as I

went across the lawn, I caught a glimpse of an old dog lying under the apple tree and saw him prick his ears and get up slowly at the sound of his mistress's voice.

Later, as we drove home, Maurice said, 'I'm sorry about that. I didn't realise the old girl would be so calm. You're the one who felt it most.'

'I was just being sentimental, Mrs Bond felt it more than I did really, but she had got things in proportion.'

That evening, after Surgery, Margaret came running into the sitting room. 'Miss Pemberton is coming up the drive with her poodles and she's got someone with her who looks exactly the same as she does, with two more poodles.'

'You're seeing double,' Maurice said, 'there's only one Miss Pemberton, thank God.'

He heaved himself out of his chair and went to the window. 'Good Lord! You're right, come and look.'

Two rather eccentric looking ladies were strolling up towards the house, each with two revoltingly fat little dogs on long leads. Miss Pemberton was dressed as usual in a vague kind of gipsy style, a shapeless skirt and a blouse with billowing sleeves, lots of dangling necklaces and a large straw hat and the other woman, to my amazement, looked like a carbon copy with almost identical clothes.

'It must be her twin sister,' I said, 'and I'm afraid this is a social call.'

Maurice groaned, 'Oh! God! What are we in for now?'

Margaret brought them into the sitting room and Miss Pemberton, tangled up with dog leads, beamed at us. 'So glad you're in. I simply had to bring my sister to meet you. She's taken a house down here so we can be together in our old age.'

She laughed girlishly, showing all her teeth, and her straw hat slipped slightly to one side as she bent to disentangle one of the dogs from the leg of a chair. 'Now, let me introduce you.' She drew her sister forward and as we shook hands, I tried to find a way of distinguishing one from the other. I was just coming to the conclusion that it was impossible when I noticed that Mrs Wittering wore a gold locket among her necklaces and that her straw hat was a little smaller than her sister's and seemed to be more firmly fixed.

'Our wonderful Vet,' Miss Pemberton was saying. 'Mozart and Haydn don't know what they would do without their dear doctor, do they?'

She gazed adoringly down at her two dogs who had clambered up into an armchair and were pushing and fighting for the best position. 'Now, that's naughty, Mozart. You mustn't take up all the chair. Let Mummy sit down first, then you can both sit on my lap.'

As Mrs Wittering settled herself in another chair, I asked, 'What are your dogs called? Are you musical, too?'

She pulled the two struggling dogs up on to her lap. 'Oh, yes. Madge and I play duets together and, do you know, our little friends here lift up their heads and sing. It's really quite remarkable. Mine are called Bach and Handel.'

I racked my brains for something nice to say about them. 'They look very intelligent.'

Mrs Wittering beamed up at me. 'You can see that at once, can't you? Bach here is sometimes very naughty and gives me a little nip occasionally but I always say his "Bach" is worse than his bite.'

I laughed dutifully, asked if they would like some coffee and, when they assented, I escaped thankfully into the kitchen. When, eventually, I returned with the tray, I saw, from the glazed look in Maurice's eyes that he had been drawn into a dog-worshipping orgy.

'See' Miss Pemberton pointed to Mozart and Haydn, aren't they bright? They knew directly you opened the door that you were bringing in some bikkies for them.'

Mrs Wittering, not to be outdone added, 'Bach and Handel were holding their little noses right up in the air. They have this wonderful sense of smell, you see. They know much more than we mere humans do, don't they, Mr Bowring?'

Maurice got up and helped me with the tray.

'Well . . .' he looked at the squirming, undisciplined animals, 'I wouldn't say they know more than humans. But some dogs are very intelligent, of course.'

'There you are,' Miss Pemberton gave her animals a playful poke, 'Doctor man says you're clever, so you must be. Now show him how you can beg for a bikkie.'

She took a biscuit from the plate on the coffee table and held it over Mozart's nose. He grabbed it from her hand and proceeded to scatter crumbs all over my armchair. 'Naughty! Naughty! You didn't beg. But *you* will, won't you, Haydn?'

'It's been a lovely summer, hasn't it?' I said, trying to change the conversation. 'Did you go away for your holiday?'

Miss Pemberton nodded enthusiastically, 'Oh, yes. We went up to Aunty's.' Then addressing herself to Mozart and Haydn, 'You had a lovely time with your cousins didn't you? And we helped Aunty to move house.' She turned to me, 'The removal men were so funny, you know, they kept pretending they didn't like dogs and called them such amusing names but, of course, it was all a big joke really. We knew they were only teasing us.'

Mrs Wittering leant forward earnestly, 'You know Madge, I wasn't too sure about that big man with the ginger hair. I thought he went a little too far sometimes. Bach didn't take to him at all.'

'That's true. Poor man.' Miss Pemberton gave a biscuit to each dog and then reached out for more.

Suddenly Maurice said, 'You know, you really shouldn't feed those dogs so much. Think of their figures – they're far too fat already.'

There was dead silence as each lady looked at the other in consternation and then at their dogs.

Then Mrs Wittering gave a tinkling laugh. 'Oh! Mr Bowring, how funny! Think of their figures, indeed! Madge said you were a great humourist – now I see what she means.'

Maurice stared at them helplessly and then half shut his eyes. Something would obviously have to be done to end this ghastly visit. What a contrast these dotty women were to the sensible old lady we had seen this afternoon! For a moment I considered telling them about her. But they would never understand. They were incurable. Somehow or other, I must get rid of them.

'I'll get some more coffee,' I said, and went quickly back to the kitchen where Margaret had taken refuge. We exchanged a few words, she nodded and then, unable to control her mirth, rushed outside. Armed with the coffee pot I returned to the sitting room and sat patiently listening to the inane conversation.

Then – glorious sound – the telephone rang and I got up quickly. Margaret's voice, coming from the call box up the road, was choked with laughter. 'Would you ask Mr Bowring to come out to see my pony? He's gone down with colic and it's urgent.'

'I'll just take the address,' I said, and then handed Maurice the slip of paper on which I had written 'Fake call from Margaret. Pretend you have to go out to see a pony with colic.'

'Oh, dear!' Maurice frowned. He looked at the two ladies engrossed in dog adoration, 'I'm so sorry. I'm going to have to break up this pleasant visit. An urgent call to a horse with colic.'

'We quite understand,' the sisters rose at once and immediately became entangled in dog leads. Mrs Wittering said she was so pleased to have met Maurice and she knew that Bach and Handel would be quite safe in his hands and if there were the teeniest-weeniest signs of anything being wrong with them, she would ring him at once and Miss Pemberton, leading the way, turned to thank me for the coffee and biscuits.

'Your husband is such a busy man, Mrs Bowring. Working day and night for the benefit of the sweet animals. You must feel proud to be able to help him. Now, come along doggies, we mustn't hold your nice doctor back from his errand of mercy.'

We waved them goodbye and, as they went down the path, Maurice walked round to the garage. A minute later he drove past them down the road and, in a very short time, he returned via the back lane.

'That was a marvellous idea,' he grinned as he came

into the kitchen where Margaret and I were washing up the coffee things and, taking a fifty-pence piece from his pocket, he handed it to Margaret. 'That's a retaining fee, I'll probably need your services again some time.'

Chapter 28

The Surgery was crowded with a variety of patients. Cats needing their injections against feline enteritis, cats with bad ears, dogs with kidney trouble, diarrhoea, rheumatism, the list of things they suffered from seemed endless.

I was not feeling at my best, having just recovered from a bout of influenza and when a large, tame rabbit with an abscess the size of an egg on its cheek became unexpectedly wild and tried madly to hop off the edge of the table, I lost my grip and my temper at the same time.

Maurice shouted, 'For heaven's sake! Hold him firmly.'

I grabbed a handful of skin on its back and held on so tightly that it gave up the struggle and I watched as Maurice froze the area around the abscess. Then, as he lanced the revolting lump, I half turned my head away and he laughed. 'After all these years you ought to be hardened.'

'I am,' I said, 'or I wouldn't be doing this. I can think of a lot more pleasant ways of spending my time.'

He finished draining the abscess and injected an antibiotic into the cavity, then he looked up at me. 'More pleasant, perhaps, but probably not so worth while.'

Still disgruntled, I shrugged my shoulders and was immediately sorry when I saw the hurt look on his face. Post influenza depression can cause one to say cruel things and I resolved to put myself on a course of vitamins.

Handing the rabbit back to the small boy in the

Waiting Room and seeing the child's face light up with relief, I began to feel better. Even such a small thing as this brought satisfaction. I was just about to call in the next patient when the door burst open and a man came in, staggering under the weight of a large dog wrapped in a blanket, followed by a woman in tears.

I recognised them as a middle-aged couple we knew quite well and my heart sank as I realised that the dog was their beloved 'Chum'. 'He's badly hurt. May we go in straight away?' Mr Loman asked and I nodded and ushered them in to Maurice.

As soon as the dog was on the table Mr Loman pulled back the blanket. 'His front paw is crushed to bits,' he said, and as I looked at the bloody, mangled mess, I felt sick with horror.

'The car went racing off,' Mrs Loman added, in a high, hysterical voice, 'we never even got the number. He came tearing round the corner of the lane, just missed us and caught Chum's foot.'

The dog, suffering from shock and pain, lay limp with only an occasional whimper and as Maurice examined it gently trying to ascertain the damage, I reached for a syringe.

Measuring out a morphine-based pain killer, Maurice gave the injection while Mrs Loman continued her tale, 'We managed to pick him up and came straight here. He bit me but he didn't know what he was doing, oh! Chum . . .'

She broke down in sobs and I led her away from the table. Wordlessly, she held out her wrist to show me the bite but it hadn't punctured the skin and was only a bad bruise.

'Sit down here,' I said, pulling out a chair, 'I'll make you a cup of tea while your husband is helping to hold Chum.'

While I was boiling the water I thought about the beautiful dog lying on the table. A magnificent red setter and a great friend of ours. He came regularly into the Surgery for a routine check-up and booster injections, his tail waving and his eyes full of friendliness. After treatment, he always handed us his front paw – the one that was now such a sorry mess – as if to show there was no hard feelings. A young dog, he kept his master and mistress healthy with the long walks they gave him every day and his coat shone with regular grooming. He was everything a dog should be, fit, well-trained and good-tempered and he brought great joy into the Lomans' otherwise rather dull existence.

I handed out the cups of hot, sweet tea and watched as they drank gratefully and the colour began to come back into their cheeks.

At last Mr Loman asked, 'What can you do, Mr Bowring?'

Maurice, who had been standing deep in thought, looked up. 'I may have to take his foot off but I'll know more when I've examined it thoroughly. I suggest you go home and wait there. I'll ring you when I've finished and tell you what I've done. The injection I've given him is taking away all pain and I'll begin on him as soon as I've finished doing this Surgery.'

He obviously wasn't going to commit himself further and, as I took them out the back way, I said, 'Try not to worry too much. At least he wasn't killed.'

When I returned Maurice told me he didn't know how

long the foot would take and he had two more operations to do as well. He wanted to get the rest of the people in the Surgery done as quickly as possible.

When, finally, I closed the door behind the last client, Maurice said, 'Right. Now let's see what we can do with Chum. He's in a state of light anaesthesia, so it will make it that much easier to examine his foot.'

The red setter was so dopy that he was quite unable to stand on his three legs and was almost a dead weight as we lifted him on to the table.

When Maurice had cleaned out the gravel and dust he took forceps and a knife and took out all the splinters of bone, then cut away the thin pieces of skin that would not heal.

'I think,' he said at last, 'I can save that one toe if I stitch it to that piece of skin and, thank goodness, the big pad underneath isn't badly damaged.'

Satisfied, he stood back and looked at me.

'No amputation?' I asked and he shook his head.

'I'm going to see if I can make up what's left here into some semblance of a foot. The big pad will take the weight, I'm sure.'

I watched spellbound as he moulded and pressed until he had a sort of ball. Then taking the suturing needle, he began to stitch and join it all to the pad. The one remaining toe had its own little pad left and he stitched and joined that to the main body.

At last, he stood upright and surveyed his work. 'That's the best I can do. I think he'll be able to walk and run eventually. I'll just pack it up with antibiotic powder while you look out a tubular bandage. When that's on I'll give him an injection to bring him round.'

The finished job looked better than I could ever have believed possible but, even then, I grieved for the Lomans. Their beautiful dog would no longer be perfect. I wondered how they would take the news.

They must have been sitting by the telephone, for they answered immediately and Maurice told them what he had done. When he put down the receiver he smiled as he turned to me. 'They're so grateful it's overwhelming. They don't mind a disfigurement so long as Chum can walk normally eventually. They had had visions of a three-legged dog and I only hope what I have done will turn out successfully. Now, let's get on with the next operation.'

The Labrador puppy with the entropion sat looking at us with his eye half closed and the bluish coloured interior could hardly be seen. It is a condition that sometimes occurs in animals and this puppy, the last of the litter, had been born with it, much to the owner's distress.

She had brought it in to the Surgery last week thinking the puppy would have to be put to sleep and, when Maurice told her he could put it right, she was overjoyed.

'It's like this,' he explained to her, 'the lower lid of the eyelid is turned in, so that the eyelashes are in direct contact with the eye. It's just a question of plastic surgery. I shall take a piece of skin, the shape of a half-moon, from below the eyelid, draw the skin together, pull the eyelid down and stitch on the piece. In about ten days, I'll take the stitches out and the pup will have a normal eye. I did this operation on a tiger cub at the Zoo only a few weeks ago and he's fine now.'

It all went exactly as he said though, when he was

cutting out the skin from below the eyelid, he warned me 'This is the tricky bit. If I take out too much, the whole eyelid will be distorted and, if I take out too little, i won't pull the eyelid down enough.'

'I think you're just saying this to make me appre hensive,' I said, but he shook his head. 'No. It's just to remind myself to be careful. It's very easy to become complacent with operations and then mistakes occur.'

The last operation was done under a local anaesthetic An old spaniel had a large haematoma in his right ear and, weighed down with the lump that had formed, the poor dog held his head completely on one side. It was rather like an enormous blood blister and had caused him much irritation and consequent shaking of his head which, of course, made matters worse.

The owner had discovered it on her return from holiday The dog had been left with a neighbour and, when Maurice heard this, he asked whether there was a cat in the house.

'Yes,' she said, 'there is. Rather a mangy old puss.'

'With mites in its ear, no doubt,' said Maurice. 'These have infected your dog's ear and made him shake his head so violently that the haematoma has developed. They grow very quickly.'

Quickly freezing the area, he lanced and drained it. Then he stitched the layers of skin together, put some powder into the ear to kill the mites and the last operation of the day was over.

The Lomans were first in the Surgery that evening and Chum, fully alert, seemed remarkably cheerful. Carrying his injured foot he stood erect, his tail waving frantically as they entered.

'Let me see him in three days' time,' said Maurice, 'and I'll change the dressing and continue this every three days until it has healed.'

Three weeks later, Maurice took off the bandage for good and, by that time, Chum had already been using his foot. At first, he tended to carry it but soon, as the muscles grew stronger, he began to forget.

A month later, we met the Lomans coming home from one of their long walks. Chum came running to greet us and Maurice bent down and examined his work.

The hair was growing well and beginning to cover the scar. Apart from the misshapen foot, he was back to normal.

'Isn't that lovely?' I said, as we went on our way. 'It must give you a nice glow of satisfaction.'

Maurice smiled, 'So you think veterinary work is worth while after all, do you?'

I remembered my depressing remarks some weeks back. 'Unpleasant at times, but quite definitely worth while.'

Chapter 29

———◆———

Autumn had set in. Not the golden days we expected with misty mornings breaking out into warm sunshine and trees resplendent in russet foliage silhouetted against clear blue skies, but a chill, wet, grey October. Small rivers ran between the furrows of the newly ploughed fields and cars splashed along the country lanes, their windscreen-wipers working overtime.

Maurice's car was almost unrecognisable, mud-caked and filthy and I looked at it with distaste as he swept into the drive at lunch time but I knew it was no use mentioning the fact. With all the autumnal farm work going on, there was no time for car cleaning and, in any case, it was futile to begin the day with a shining vehicle when, in an hour or two, it would be dirty again.

He stood in the doorway, rain dripping from his hat brim and carrying his wellington boots which he took over to my newly cleaned kitchen sink.

'Just get a bit of this muck off,' he said, and I watched as the water turned black and thick but I still didn't complain. Patient Griselda has nothing on me when Maurice is occupied with tuberculin testing, brucellosis testing and all the work that goes on at this time of the year. Not only is it physically hard but it often means receiving occasional kicks from resentful cows, urine splashes from discourteous cows and malodorous clothes from all manner of unpleasant happenings. Nature is very raw at times and cows with gleaming coats in a sunny meadow are very different when packed together in a yard.

'Sorry about that,' said Maurice, trying vainly to clean up the mess in the sink having realised too late that he could easily have turned the hose on to his boots before he came indoors. But I gave what I hoped was a forgiving smile and helped him off with his coat.

'Hard morning?' I asked.

'An absolute rodeo.'

He went to pour out a drink and stood waiting as I laid the table. As a concession to the weather I had made a thick, warming soup which he was soon devouring. A snack lunch followed as usual, because, as he has said for years, he simply cannot work in the afternoon on top of a heavy meal.

'I was doing the brucellosis test at Water Farm and his herdsman is down with 'flu, so he and I and his young son just had to cope as best we could. Fifty cows all tied up as he hasn't got a crush. I had to take the blood sample from the tail and, if that failed and they jumped around too much, then I had to weave my way through them to get the needle into the jugular vein. It was sheer chaos. It took double the time it would have done if he had been properly organised. He really ought to employ another man but he can't afford to. I only hope that his herd will pass the test.'

'It's still a voluntary scheme, isn't it?' I asked.

'Yes, but it's been going on for some time now and it will soon be compulsory. The idea is to get all the herds in the country cleared so that we can wipe out contagious abortion just as we've done with tuberculosis. Brucellosis also causes undulant fever in humans.'

He paused, 'By the way, I'm booked to do Mr Thorne's tuberculin test on Tuesday, with the second one on Friday. Mrs Thorne usually takes down the details but she's got her new grandchild staying with her. Do you think you could come along?'

'Always available, that's me,' I said, mentally re-arranging my work and putting off a hairdressing appointment.

'What a life of leisure you lead,' Maurice grinned, and I saw that his face was smeared with something I preferred not to analyse.

'Before you go any further, you must wash your face. You should have done it when you came in. It's putting me off my coffee.'

'Nothing puts you off your coffee,' Maurice got up and stared at himself in the mirror. 'It's only a splash from an evil minded cow.' He wiped it off with his handkerchief.

'I'll have a good clean-up before I go out again. Now, Thorne's test will go on till early afternoon so Mrs Thorne is giving us lunch. It will be a quick one, of course, but she always puts on a pretty good meal.'

'I like that,' I said indignantly, 'I thought you said you didn't want a heavy meal at midday.'

'No choice. The other men do, so once in a while I indulge.'

On Tuesday morning, directly after Surgery, we set off for the farm. The dogs came running out to greet us as we drove in and parked the car against the wall – well away from any possible breakaway cows – and went straight to the large cowshed.

The yard outside was packed with cows milling around, bellowing mildly in protest at this change in their routine, pushing and shoving and leaving enormous dung pats everywhere which, under the heavy rain, soon became thick, brown puddles.

Mr Thorne had put a chair and a folding table up for me at the end of the cowshed, just opposite the crush, and I installed myself there armed with ruled sheets of paper and a pen and waited for the first arrival.

It was all well organised. Each cow was brought into the crush which was a tubular steel affair with two sides, a door at the far end and a yoke to hold the animal's neck. Maurice was stationed just by the yoke and, as each cow entered, the man working the yoke called out the ear number and age of the animal which I wrote down. Then Maurice clipped two patches of hair from the neck and, with a pair of calipers, he measured the double thickness of the skin and called out his reading. After that, he injected avian tuberculin into the top patch and bovine tuberculin into the lower one. After seventy-two hours – this would be done on the Friday – any consequent swelling would be measured and, from that reading, the animal is declared Passed, Failed or Doubtful. The doubtful ones would have to be retested in sixty days' time.

As soon as the injections were given and the measurements noted, the door was opened and the cow went into an enclosure at the back of the yard.

Everything went well for the first twenty minutes, then a heifer managed to get right through the crush before the gate was shut and joined the ones who had been done. This caused a certain amount of shouting and confusion whilst the men tried to separate her from her companions without success and, in the end, they all had to pass through the crush again until the guilty one was found.

Otherwise it was a monotonous job and after the first few jokes, we all settled down, trying to get it done as quickly as possible. But there was no chance to relax. This information had to be given to the Ministry of Agriculture and must be correct in every detail.

We worked at the rate of about fifty cows to the hour and by lunch time only eighty cows remained to be tested.

The rain had stopped as we came into the yard and went across to the kitchen where Mrs Thorne was waiting. Time to wash our hands; then, in a flash, plates laden with a glorious steak and kidney pie were put in front of us. Potatoes in their jackets and vegetables from the garden were handed round and the fragrant, appetising smell made me realise how hungry I was.

The dogs had followed us into the warm kitchen and were lying quietly by the stove. Mr Thorne, sitting back after having demolished an enormous helping of pudding – apple crumble topped with thick cream – looked down at them and said, 'That old dog of mine is worth his weight in gold. He brought all the cattle up from that lower field this morning entirely on his own and never lost a single one.'

His son, a big young man in his twenties, laughed scornfully, 'Your Ned takes twice as long as Jake'. He bent down and patted the smaller of the two black and white collies, 'He races round the field and brings them up to me in half the time.'

'He's too quick by far,' retorted his father, 'he nips their heels and frightens the in-calf heifers, then he waits at the gate for you to bring them up into the yard. But there – you can't expect too much of him, he's not very bright.'

I looked from one to the other, then seeing the expectant grins on the faces around the table, I realised that this was an old argument. Rivalry between father and son was being worked out in this competition between their dogs.

'He's very intelligent,' Dave's colour rose. 'He knows he isn't expert yet, that's why he comes up to me to be told what to do next.'

'And who does it in the end?' Mr Thorne snorted derisively. 'Who does it? Your Jake or you? That dog ought to be doing it on his own by now, like Ned here.' He appealed to his wife, 'You agree with me, don't you, Mother?'

Mrs Thorne smiled at me, 'Men! They're always trying to beat each other. As for the dogs – well – they both bring a lot of dirt into the house but which is the most intelligent I'm sure I don't know.' She paused, 'Let's get Mr Bowring to tell us. He knows all about animals.'

'You've put me in a hole, haven't you?' Maurice looked at the dogs sitting up now, aware that they were being discussed, 'Well, I'll give you my verdict. I think Dave's dog is the most intelligent.'

'What!' Mr Thorne looked at him incredulously and Dave gave a shout of triumph, shaking his hands together over his head like a boxer.

Maurice grinned at the company. 'I base my judgment on this: any dog that can make its master do half its work must, in my opinion, be intelligent. Highly intelligent.'

To the accompaniment of shouts of laughter we went back to the cowshed. It was then that I realised the truth of Maurice's statement that it was difficult to work after a heavy meal. The remaining eighty cows seemed to take twice as long as the morning ones and I was very thankful when the last animal passed through the crush.

'It won't take so long on Friday,' said Maurice, as we drove home, 'I only have to read the measurements so we'll probably get away before lunch. By the way,' he turned and smiled at me, 'I haven't thanked you for being so long-suffering. I know the autumn work is always difficult but this must have been the last straw.'

Gazing out of the car window, I saw that the rain clouds were moving away. Any moment now we would be having a frost and the muddy fields and lanes would dry up, making things easier all round.

'That's all right,' I said, 'you're welcome. Anyway, I think the weather is changing so I'll soon be back to normal.'

'That sounds ominous, what does it mean?'

'It means, that I'll snap your head off if you clean your wellington boots in the sink and forget to wash before you sit down to table.'

Chapter 30

We were invited to a wedding. Bill and Mary were getting married in November and it was going to take place at her parents' home in Somerset. No great distance and we could easily drive there and back in one day.

But, directly I showed the invitation to Maurice, I saw how difficult it was going to be to make him take time off from his work.

'On a Saturday? Our two busiest Surgeries? No, it's not on. You, John and Margaret will have to go without me. I can't possibly manage it.'

'Oh, yes, you can, if you try. You'll have to get a Locum. Dick will come, I've no doubt.' Then I remembered. Of course, Dick would be at the wedding, probably in the capacity of best man.

Maurice saw my dismay. 'Exactly. Dick won't be available and there's no one else who could stand in just for one day. In any case, you know how I feel about unknown Locums.'

'But you must come,' I was growing exasperated, 'we've got to think of something.'

'Like circularising all the clients known and unknown, who might turn up that Saturday?' Maurice asked sarcastically.

'Don't be ridiculous. Look – life isn't worth living if we can't have any social life at all. Now, you haven't any operations fixed that far ahead and you can avoid making any appointments for that day, so there's one thing out of the way.'

'Leaving me with the long Saturday morning Surgery, the evening one, and all the calls in between. Who's going to do all that? No. It's as I said. There's nothing to stop you and the children going but you must count me out.'

He went away and I was left reflecting angrily on the disadvantages of a one man Practice. If we had a partner or an assistant this kind of situation would never arise.

I picked up the *Veterinary Record* and scanned the advertisements. Sometimes there were people willing to do weekend Locums but, even as I ran my eye down the columns, I knew it was no use. Maurice had dug his toes in and the only thing to do was to cut away the ground from under his feet.

All that day I pondered, then at last I had the glimmering of an idea. We have a very good relationship with the Vets in neighbouring Practices and sometimes they will stand in for each other if one of them wants to go out for an evening. I thought of a Practice not far from us and felt sure that they would look after any emergencies for us if we made arrangements for the telephone to be put through to them. But when I mentioned it to Maurice, he said, 'And what about the Surgeries? All the Vets round here have their Surgeries at the same time.'

Once more I was defeated. There was only one thing for me to do. That evening, I got out my writing pad and said, 'You're absolutely certain then? You won't be going to the wedding?'

Maurice nodded, 'I'm sorry. It's too difficult.'

'O.K., I'd better write and tell them we can't manage it.'

'What do you mean? *You* can go – there's nothing to stop you. I can do the Surgeries on my own for once.'

'If you don't go then we won't,' I said firmly, 'and I must say I'm awfully disappointed. I would have enjoyed it so much.'

Maurice looked at me hard and there was a long silence. 'I'm being blackmailed!'

I said nothing and he stared at me grimly. Then he turned and went out of the room.

I settled down and wrote to Mary's parents, thanking them and explaining that we would not be able to attend the wedding and put the unstamped letter on the table where it could be plainly seen and hoped for the best.

Some time later I heard the click of the telephone and realised that someone was using it upstairs. Soon, Maurice came into the room. 'You haven't posted your letter yet, have you?' he asked and then caught sight of it on the table. 'Ah! I see you haven't got a stamp. Didn't you know there were some in the box?'

I shook my head and waited.

'Well,' he said at last, 'there's no need to post it after all. I've been in touch with Peter Rallton. He's just taken on an assistant and he's very kindly offered to lend him to us for the Surgeries and they'll both look after the day-time calls for me.'

'Why, that's marvellous, what a good idea. I never thought of that.'

'Hmm!' Maurice looked at me steadily. 'Hen-pecked! That's what I am. Pushed around and manipulated. I can't call my soul my own.'

'A little social life will do you the world of good,' I said.

The day of the wedding was bright and frosty and the drive down to Somerset was delightful. The marriage took place in a lovely old village church and Mary made a most beautiful bride. Bill was so overcome with his luck that he was almost speechless and only really came to life when someone made a speech and mentioned that it was the happy couple's mutual love of pigs that had brought them together.

On our way home Maurice said, 'Bill is in luck. I had a few words with him before they went away and he told me his father-in-law has promised that eventually he and Mary can take over his farm.'

I was delighted. 'That's wonderful. Do you know, I feel a bit responsible for that marriage. After all, I did make him bring her down to the farm.'

'Oh, I don't know, Mary would have got him in the end, anyway. When a woman makes up her mind she usually gets what she wants. By fair means or foul. Which reminds me,' he glanced at me sideways, 'there's a price to pay for this unaccustomed freedom today. When Peter offered his assistant to do my work we got talking about our families and he mentioned that his wife was fed-up because she had been inveigled into helping with some local bazaar. Although she made the usual excuse, saying that as a Vet's wife she was too busy, she hasn't been able to get out of it. So I suggested you should do it instead. She's terribly grateful and is coming to see you soon and give you all the details.'

I sat stunned into silence and Maurice patted my shoulder encouragingly, 'You'll enjoy it. After all, being a

Vet's wife needn't take up all your time. You must have a little social life occasionally.'

'One of the few advantages of this work,' I said coldly, 'is that up till now I have been able to get out of doing things I don't want to do. Like helping with bazaars, for instance.'

Then I began to laugh, 'You'll live to regret it, I'll probably buy your Christmas present there.'

We arrived home at a reasonable hour and sat for a while talking about the wedding. When, at last, it was time for Maurice to take the dog out for his nightly walk before going to bed, he stood for a moment at the open door.

'It's a beautiful night, how about putting on your coat and coming with me?'

The moon was full and everything was quiet under a glistening frost. We walked up the lane and then stood for a while at a gate, looking across the white fields.

'Just like the night we got engaged,' said Maurice, 'sometimes it seems only yesterday. We hardly knew each other and I wasn't even qualified. Do you wish now that I hadn't become a Vet?'

'Of course I don't. I know I grumble at times but, really, I love the life we lead, I couldn't be happier.'

'Nor could I,' said Maurice.